DEAR RE ERS

The greeting is right, you are not mistaken. You must have thought this is an ordinary book with some exciting content about physics, but this special book is much MORE than that!

WHAT MAKES THIS HYBRID BOOK SPECIAL?

In addition to being fascinating to read, this hybrid media publication also includes 3D videos. Every chapter contains cutting-edge augmented reality technology; The physical phenomena comes to life in AR animations on a mobile device.

SNEAK PEEK...

What do we know about motion? What is angular momentum? What does friction mean? How do the lever, the wave wheel, and the mirror work? What are the characteristics of waves? What do we need to know about electricity? All exciting questions from everyday life – presented in an unconventional way and with spectacular animations!

A GUIDE FOR USING THE AR CONTENT

1. Download the **AR Books LibrARy** app.

arbookslibrary.com/app

Download on the App Store

GET IT ON Google Play

2. Register and log in.

3. Follow the instructions in the app.

4. Book ID:

PHENOMENA

We wish you an enjoyable reading & cinema experience!

The authors and the developers

1 UNIFORM & RECTILINEAR

In motion processes, the position of bodies changes relative to a reference system. If the distance travelled by the body is straight and its velocity does not change, the movement is said to be rectilinear and uniform. The movement of a bubble in an inclined Mikola tube is also of this type if the angle of inclination does not change.

QUICKNESS

*Constant speed in uniform motion means that the distance travelled by a body is directly proportional to the time it takes to travel that distance. The ratio between the distance **s** covered and the time **t** needed to cover it is the velocity **v**, which is derived from the Latin word "velocitas" (speed): **v = s/t**. In many cases, the speed is calculated from a part of the total distance travelled (**Δs**), and the time it takes to cover it (**Δt**): **v = Δs/Δt**.*

Velocity

DIMENSIONS

A uniform rectilinear motion is achieved when the forces acting on the moving body are eliminated or balanced. The sum of the forces acting on the body is zero: **ΣF = 0N**. The SI unit of the resulting speed is the ratio of metres to seconds (m/s), but kilometres per hour (km/h) is more commonly used in everyday life. The conversion between the two units is as follows:

$$1\frac{m}{s} = 1\frac{\frac{1}{1000}\,km}{\frac{1}{3600}\,h} = \frac{3600}{1000}\frac{km}{h} = 3.6\frac{km}{h}$$

$$1\frac{km}{h} = 1\frac{1000\,m}{3600\,s} = \frac{10}{36}\frac{m}{s} \approx 0.2778\frac{m}{s}$$

WHICH IS FASTER?

Since speed is the distance travelled in one second, distance is in direct proportion to time at a constant speed (**$s = v \cdot t$**). If you plot the distance as a function of time, you get a line whose gradient corresponds to the speed of the body. A higher speed means that the distance travelled within the same time period is greater, so the slope of the line in the distance-time graph is also greater. The graph in the illustration shows the relation between speed and time of three objects: **$v_1 > v_2 > v_3$**.

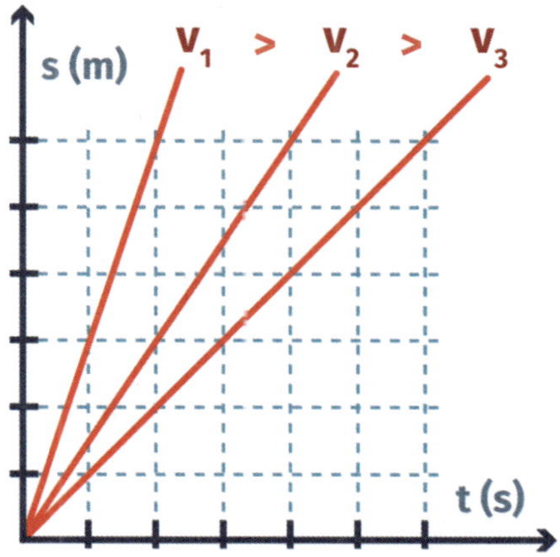

Distance-time graph

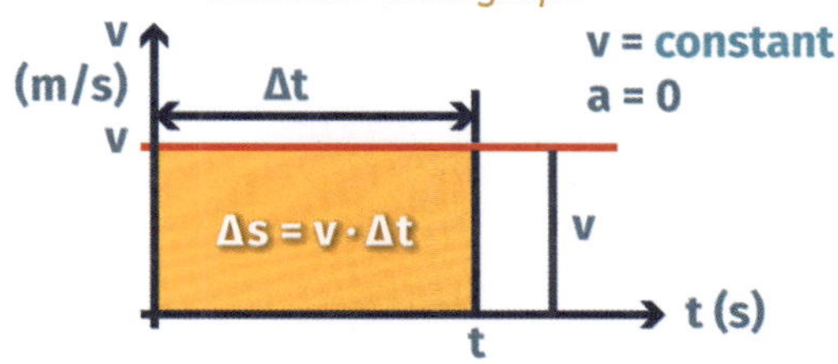

Velocity-time graph

UNDER THE CURVE

If we also draw the velocity-time graph, the result is a horizontal line, since there is no force acting on the body that could cause acceleration or deceleration. The product of the constant velocity and the elapsed time gives the area of the rectangle under the "curve" that corresponds exactly to the **distance travelled by the body**. It is worth noting that the area under the curve of the velocity-time graph can be used to provide the value of the distance travelled by the body for any type of movement besides the uniform motion.

2 ACCELERATION / DECELERATION

Starting and ending a movement is only possible by applying force: the velocity of the body has to be increased or decreased. The rate of change of velocity is called acceleration and, as an abbreviation of the Latin word "acceleratio", it is indicated by the letter "a".

ACCELERATION

We speak of a uniformly accelerated rectilinear motion if the trajectory of the motion is straight and the change in velocity is proportional to the time elapsed. Acceleration shows the velocity change of the body in one second. Its unit of measurement can be derived from the following equation.

$$a = \frac{\Delta v}{\Delta t} \Rightarrow \frac{m}{s^2}$$

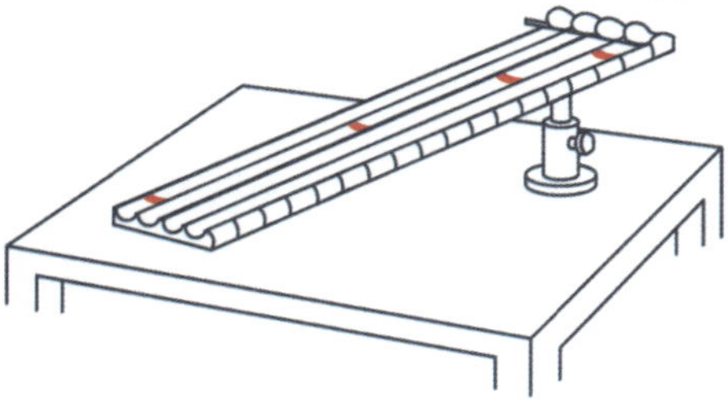

Galileo ramp

Acceleration is a change in velocity

DEMONSTRATION

The phenomenon of acceleration can be visualised by the **Galileo ramp**, where four initially stationary balls placed side by side are simultaneously released, each of which collides with a bell at the end of their trajectory. The trajectory of each ball is set at a different length in such a way that the first one should be the shortest, and the fourth the longest, in order that the accelerating balls will hit the bells at equal time intervals. It is only possible if the length of their trajectories does not increase uniformly, but at a rate of 1:4:9:16.

$$s = \frac{a}{2} \cdot t^2$$

PLOTTED ON GRAPHS

When you start a body from a stationary position with constant acceleration, its velocity will increase uniformly, and the velocity-time graph will be straight. The slope of the line is equal to the acceleration (**$\Delta v = a \cdot \Delta t$**). The consequence of the increase in velocity is that the distance travelled in one second will increase continuously. The distance travelled is therefore a quadratic function of the time elapsed, and the distance-time graph is a parabola.

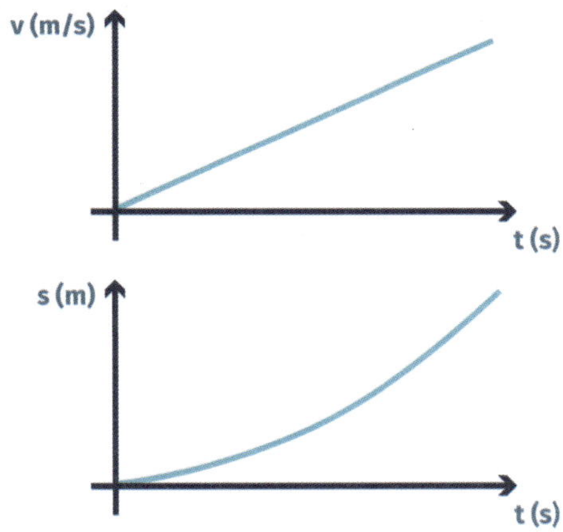

Velocity – time & distance – time graph

WHAT IS IT CAUSED BY?

Acceleration requires a force, and force is a vector quantity, thus acceleration is also a vector quantity. In addition to its magnitude, its direction is also important. In rectilinear motion, both the acceleration and velocity vectors are parallel to the direction of the movement. The accelerating force can be generated by human means, by an electric or internal combustion engine, by using the force of gravity, by magnetic or electric fields, but it can also be caused by friction and drag.

DECELERATION IS ALSO AN ACCELERATION

3

DROP THE BALL

Free fall is a special case of uniformly accelerated rectilinear motion, where the initial velocity is zero, and the path of motion is vertical. In a vertical throw, the body already has an initial velocity and therefore moves upwards. The acceleration vector is of the same magnitude in both cases and is directed downwards.

GRAVITATIONAL ACCELERATION

Gravitational acceleration (**g**) can also be determined from Newton's law by the gravitational force and the mass of the body. The value of acceleration is the quotient of these two quantities, about 9.81 m / s² on Earth, which means that when **falling freely**, the speed of the body increases by 9.81 m / s – equivalent to 36 km / h – per second.

Free fall

LET'S GIVE IT A TRY!

Balls of the same size, released simultaneously from the same height will land at the same time, regardless of their mass and material. However, when a feather is dropped simultaneously with an iron ball, the feather will take longer to land. The reason for this is **air resistance** (the drag of the air), which is much greater for the feather with its large surface area compared to its small mass.

LET'S MEASURE IT

The greater the mass of two bodies and the closer they are, the greater the **gravitational force** occurs between them. In the Earth's gravitational field, the value of gravitational acceleration depends on the geographical location and the altitude. For example, in London, the acceleration is 9.81 m / s^2, but in New York it is 9.80 m / s^2. In free fall, in the equations for uniformly accelerated motion with zero initial velocity, **g** is used in place of the acceleration **a**, and height **h** for the distance:

$$h=\frac{g}{2}\cdot t^2 \quad v=g\cdot t \quad t=\sqrt{\frac{2h}{g}}$$

LET'S THROW IT VERTICALLY

*Vertical throwing means that a body is thrown upwarcs and then we examine the movement it makes. Gravity acts on it in the same way as on the droppec body, but first, its initial velocity (**v_0**) is reduced. In the meantime, it elevates more and more slowly and finally stops after a time **$t = v_0/g$** The maximum height (**v_{max}**) can be determined by the following equation for uniformly accelerated rectilinear motions with an initial velocity not equal to zero.*

$$y=v_0\cdot t-\frac{g}{2}\cdot t^2$$

THE VERTICALLY THROWN STONE ELEVATES FOR THE SAME AMOUNT OF TIME AS IT FALLS

4

THE BIG SHOT

When we throw a ball to one of our teammates, we may as well do it horizontally. It cannot be noticed at a short distance, but if we are further apart, we can see the ball moving downwards as it gets farther and farther, or it can even fall to the ground. The reason for this, of course, is nothing but gravity, which acts on moving bodies in the same way.

GRAVITY INTERVENES

It can be observed that the higher the **horizontal speed** of the throw is, the faster the thrown ball hits the target. In other words, gravity has "less time" to exert its effect and deflect the ball from the target by accelerating it downwards. A faster throw can therefore be more accurate in this case.

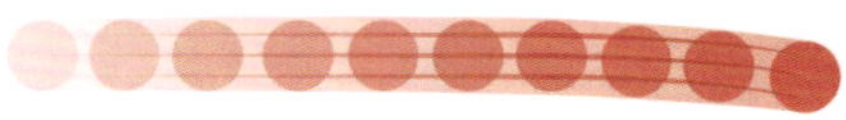

Go for it!

AIM ACCURATELY

No matter how much the horizontal velocity is increased, the trajectory of the body can never remain horizontal. Even with firearms with a bullet velocity of over 1000 m / s, hitting the target aimed at cannot be granted. Therefore, adjust your aim slightly above the target. This is called **elevation**, the value of which depends on the distance, the horizontal velocity, as well as any interfering factors (e.g., wind speed).

This trajectory will not be horizontal either

THE SUM OF VECTORS

The motion of a horizontally thrown body is described as the sum of a horizontal motion with constant velocity and a vertically **accelerated motion**, the free fall. This is possible because gravity does not change the magnitude of the horizontal velocity and a body set in motion horizontally has no initial velocity in the vertical direction. The resulting vector, which is the sum of the two velocity vectors, always points at the tangential direction of the movement path.

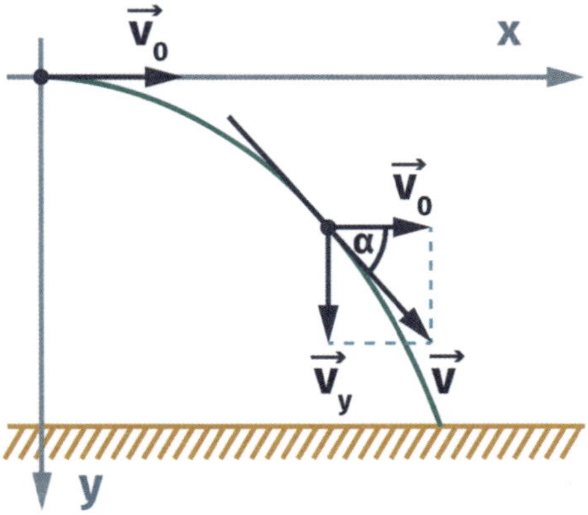

The sum is the tangent

THE WATERFALL

One such special case is a waterfall, where the constant horizontal velocity of a river or stream is accompanied by free fall. In this case, the horizontal velocity is constant $\mathbf{v_x = v_0}$*, while the vertical velocity increases continuously according to the equation* $\mathbf{v_y = g \cdot t}$*. The amount of the instantaneous velocity (**v**) can be calculated by using the Pythagorean theorem. The resulting trajectory of the falling water is parabolic.*

$$v^2 = v_x^2 + v_y^2 = v_0^2 + g^2 \cdot t^2$$

THE TRAJECTORY OF THE HORIZONTAL THROW IS NOT HORIZONTAL

5 ROUND AND ROUND

As all points of a circle are equidistant from its centre, a motion involving a rotation around a given point is called circular motion. A circular motion can have a constant velocity, i.e., it can be uniform, or variable velocity, i.e., accelerating.

UNIFORM MOTION

The clock hands also perform a uniform circular motion. It takes one hour for the large hand to complete a full revolution, 12 hours for the small hand and one minute for the second hand. After one revolution, the movement is repeated, so the circular movement is **periodic**. The time needed for one revolution is the period (**T**), the number of turns per second is the frequency (**f**).

The hands on the clock go round and round...

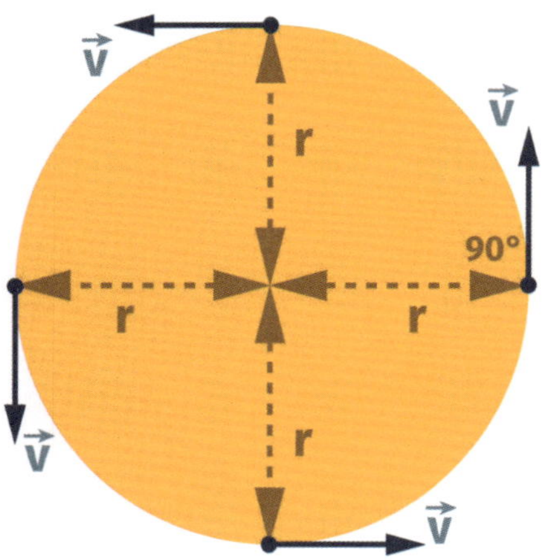

Here, the magnitude of the velocity is the same, but its direction is different

TANGENTIAL DIRECTION

In the case of circular motion, the distance travelled is the arc travelled on the circular path, and the current speed is the speed in the direction of the tangent of the circle, and it is called the **circumferential speed**. Another important characteristic is the angle of rotation of the radius drawn to a point moving on the arc. The unit of measurement of that is the radian, which shows the ratio of the radius and the length of the arc travelled. Since the circumference of the circle is $C = 2r\pi$, the radius fits the circumference exactly 2π times, i.e., **360°** equals to 2π radians.

CLOSER MEANS SLOWER

The relation between the length of the arc travelled **Δs** and the angular displacement **$\Delta\alpha$** is **$\Delta s = r \cdot \Delta\alpha$** if the angle is measured in radians. The circumferential speed is the arc length travelled in one second.

$$v_c = \frac{\Delta s}{\Delta t}$$

The angular displacement per unit of time is the angular velocity (**ω**).

$$\omega = \frac{\Delta\alpha}{\Delta t}$$

Its unit of measurement is the angular displacement divided by time, i.e., radians / second or 1 / s. The circumferential speed depends on the radius and the angular velocity as well.

$$v_c = r \cdot \omega$$

WITH TWO TYPES OF ACCELERATION

Since during circular motion the direction of velocity is constantly changing, and a change in velocity is caused by acceleration, there is always acceleration. The radial component of the acceleration of a body moving on a circular path is the centripetal acceleration, which is always pointing at the centre of the circle. Its formula is:

$$a_{cp} = \frac{v_c^2}{r} = \omega^2 \cdot r$$

The tangential component of the acceleration is called the circumferential or tangential acceleration. It increases the circumferential and angular velocities.

Smaller radius results in lower speed

6 SWIRL AND SPIN

In progressive motion, momentum is an important quantity, which is the product of the mass and velocity of the body. Based on this, angular momentum, also known as rotational momentum, can be defined for circular motion. It should be noted that the points of a rotating body do not move at the same speed.

LET'S EXAMINE IT IN MORE DETAIL

The figure skater suddenly starts to spin like crazy, seemingly without any help. How can he do so? The difference in velocity is due to the fact that before he starts spinning, he stretches both his arms out to the sides and then pulls them closer and closer to his body. This changes **the arrangement of his body's points**. The angular momentum remains the same, while the angular velocity increases.

$$\Theta = \sum_i m_i \cdot r_i^2$$

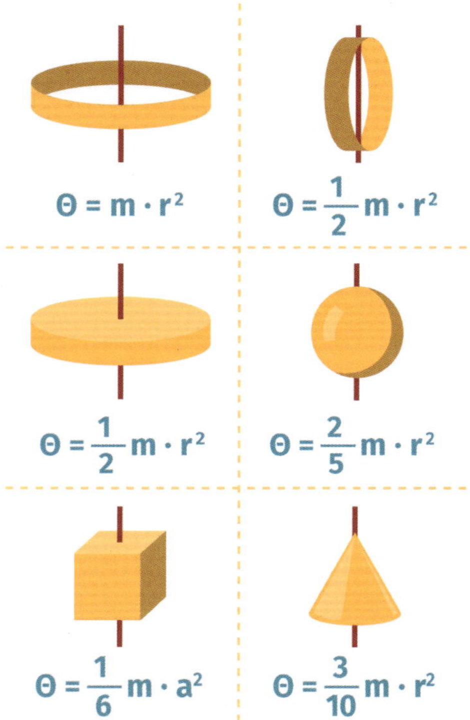

Moments of inertia of some bodies with respect to the axis shown in red

INERTIA

The resistance of a rigid body to a torque is characterised by the **moment of inertia**, which depends on the shape of the body, its mass distribution, and the position of the axis of rotation. Its symbol is **Θ** (theta), and its unit is kgm^2. The greater the mass of the point particle, but even more so, the greater its distance from the axis of rotation the greater its moment of inertia. If each point particle is considered individually with its mass (**m_i**) and distance (**r_i**), the sum of the moments of inertia of all points gives the value for the entire body.

LET'S DEMONSTRATE

The angular momentum of a rotating body (**N**) is the product of the body's moment of inertia and its angular velocity: $N = \Theta \cdot \omega$. The greater the angular momentum of a rotating body is, the more difficult it is to stop it. The **angular momentum** is a vector quantity, which can be demonstrated with an experiment. When we sit on a swivel chair, the spinning wheel in our hand will not turn us around until the axes of the disc and the wheel are in line.

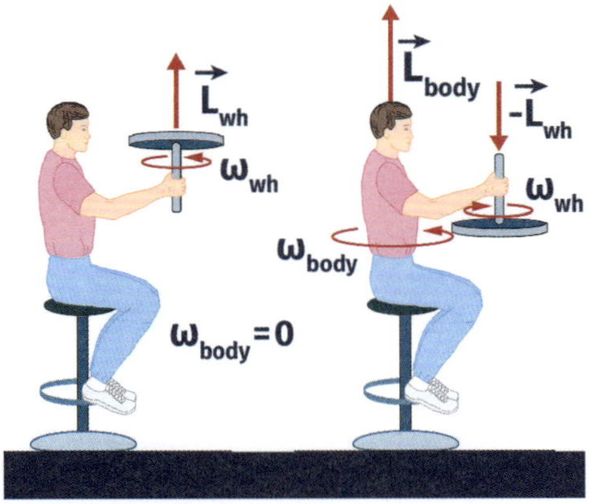

Experiment

WHAT MIGHT CHANGE IT?

*A change in the angular momentum of a rigid body (a system of point particles) can only occur through the exertion of torque. According to the law of angular momentum, the change in the total angular momentum (**ΔN**) of a system of point particles divided by the time elapsed (**Δt**) is equal to the sum of the external torques acting on the system (**ΣM**). The outcome is the law of conservation of angular momentum stating that the total angular momentum of a closed system of point particles (**$\Sigma M_i=0$**) is constant (**ΔN=0**):*

$$\sum_i M_i = \frac{\Delta N}{\Delta t} \Rightarrow \frac{\Delta N}{\Delta t} = 0$$

While rotating, it does not tip over

7 GOOD VIBES

Vibrations or oscillations are movements that repeat between two end points of a path. Oscillations can be periodic or chaotic, harmonic or disharmonic, damped or undamped. For example, when a body attached to a spring is displaced from its equilibrium position, it oscillates harmonically.

OSCILLATORY MOTION

Oscillatory motion can be performed by a point particle, a rigid body, or a medium, but also by periodic changes in electric and magnetic fields. A point on a waving surface of water, a guitar string, the membrane of a loudspeaker, or a bouncing ball all make oscillatory motion.

The tuning fork vibrates and so does the air

IN NUMERICAL TERMS

The distance between the equilibrium position of the oscillation and its endpoint is the **amplitude** of the oscillation. Its symbol is **A**. The distance between the two endpoints of the path of vibrational motion is the **peak-to-valley value of the oscillation**. The time required for an oscillation to run through its entire course once is the **period**. Its symbol is **T**, and its unit of measurement is the second (**s**). The reciprocal of the period is the **frequency** (**f**), which is the number of **oscillations** per unit time, with the unit of measurement Hz (hertz).

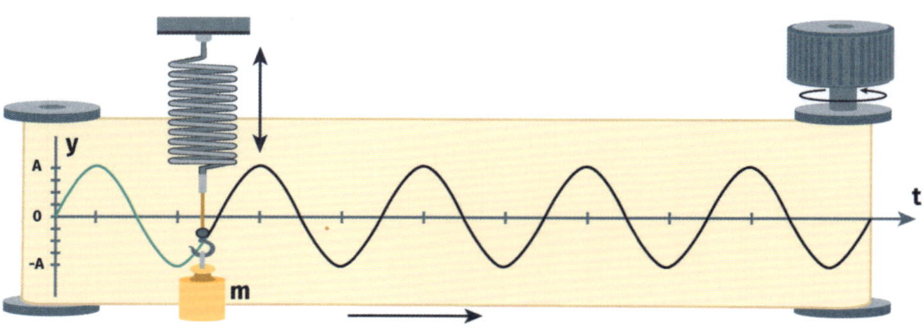

Harmonic oscillation – sinusoidal displacement

TRANSFORMED

Harmonic oscillation is a periodic motion related to a uniform circular motion. If a body makes a uniform circular motion along a circle of radius **R** whose centre is also the origin of a Cartesian coordinate system **xy**, and only the body's displacement in the vertical (**y**) direction and its velocity are considered, the **origin** can be regarded as the **equilibrium position**, the **y** coordinate as the **instantaneous displacement** and the radius **R** as the **amplitude A** of the oscillation.

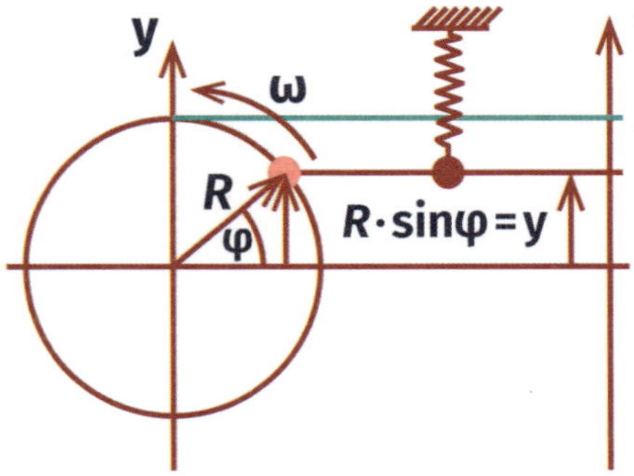

Vertical component

AS A FUNCTION

It is therefore true for both circular and oscillatory movements that the instantaneous position of the point particle can be measured by its angular movement. In case of uniform motion, the phase angle φ *is directly proportional to the time* $\varphi(t) = \omega \cdot t$, *where the proportionality factor is the angular velocity* $\omega = 2\pi \cdot f$. *The instantaneous displacement measured at time* **t** *corresponds to the vertical component of the circular motion:* $y(t) = A \cdot \sin\varphi(t) = A \cdot \sin(\omega \cdot t)$. *Maximum velocity is reached when passing through the equilibrium position:* $v_{max} = A \cdot \omega$, *while acceleration is at a maximum at the endpoint:* $a_{max} = A \cdot \omega^2$.

THE VIBRATION OF A MOBILE PHONE IS GENERATED BY AN ELECTRIC MOTOR

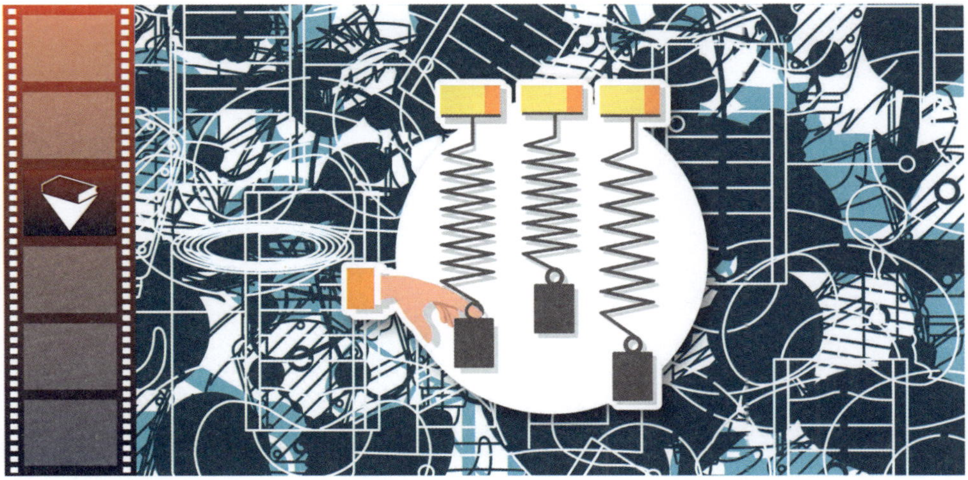

8

STATIC AND KINETIC

Trying to move a heavy object, we find that a small force does not move it. And when a greater force is applied, it is much more difficult to get it to start moving from a standstill than to keep it moving. This is because the static friction between the object and the ground is greater than the kinetic friction.

USEFULLY

Not even one step could be made without the static friction between the ground and our feet. It is also the force of static friction between the tire and the asphalt that makes turning a car possible. Without static friction, bodies would only stay in place on a perfectly horizontal surface and would start moving and sliding at the slightest inclination. Even the use of shoelaces requires friction.

EVEN SCREWS WOULD NOT HOLD WITHOUT FRICTION

MEASURABLE FORCES

The **static friction force** prevents bodies at rest from being set in motion. Its maximum value can be measured by measuring the maximum force at the time immediately before the movement starts. A force gauge is used to measure the **kinetic** force on the body pulled evenly on the table. Both frictional forces depend on the roughness of the two surfaces, and the force that presses the surfaces together (gravity in our case).

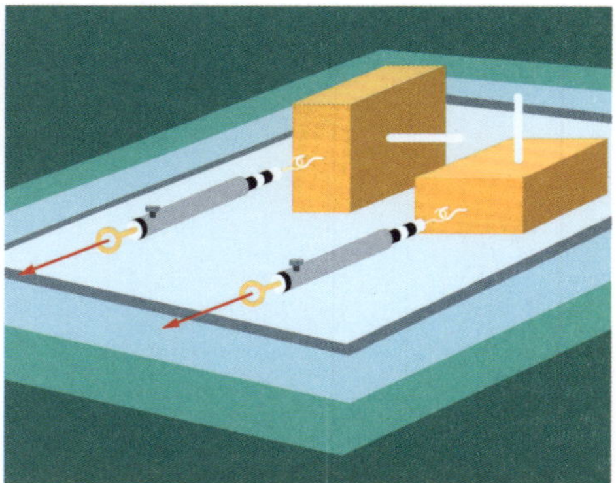

Friction is independent of the size of the surface area in contact between the moving bodies

HEATING

Static and kinetic friction forces occur at the **contact surface** of two objects, but displacement occurs only during sliding, but **work is performed** only in the latter case. In many cases, there is also a breaking of certain chemical bonds at the contact surfaces, which requires energy. The heat generated can also be utilised.

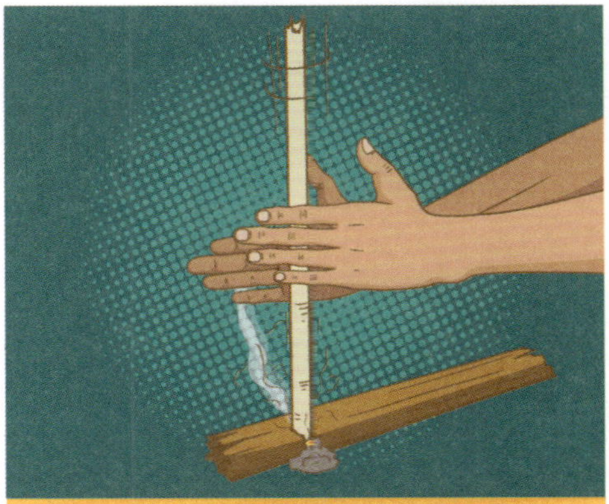

Let's use it

Stop!

UTILISATION

Friction is usually considered a **loss**; however, it can also be utilised for several things. It is important for not only **starting** and **accelerating** movements, but also when **braking**. The friction force is given by the formula $F_f = \mu \cdot F_n$, where μ is the coefficient of friction depending on the materials and F_n is the normal force. To increase the frictional force, in addition to roughening the surfaces, an increase in the normal force can also be applied.

9 RESISTANCE OF MEDIA

The resistance of a medium can be illustrated in a simple way. Let us move our hands quickly from side to side! We will feel the air hindering our movement. If we repeat this in water, for example in a swimming pool, the hindering effect can be felt even more prominently.

WHAT HINDERS US?

We often find that the medium around us makes it difficult to move, depending on our speed. Overcoming the resistance of a medium can be very strenuous, for example, when running in water or cycling into a headwind. Resistance of a medium is therefore a phenomenon that occurs when moving in a fluid or air.

The velocity is the most decisive

THE MEDIUM CAN HINDER, BUT IT CAN ALSO HELP

The resistance of the medium must also be overcome

THE MAGNITUDE OF THE FORCE

Resistance of a medium causes a force with a direction that **hinders** movement relative to the medium. The magnitude of the force depends on the velocity of the moving body relative to the medium, the shape of the body, and the density of the medium. The **drag force** is given by the formula $F_D = C_D \cdot A \cdot \rho \cdot v^2$, where v is the relative velocity of the body and the medium, C_D is the drag coefficient of the moving body, A is the cross-sectional area of the frontal surface of the body, and ρ (rho) is the density of the medium.

THE INCREASE IN VELOCITY

From the previous equation, it can be deduced that the drag force **increases quadratically** with velocity, and that a denser medium also means greater resistance. With a more favourable design, streamlined shape, or smaller frontal area, the resistance can be reduced. To reduce drag, the skier tries to adopt a body position so that he has the smallest possible surface area in the direction of movement, thus decreasing the drag coefficient the most favourably.

Shape is also important

PROGRESS

During movements, resistance of the media can also be useful. When cycling, a tailwind helps you move forward, since the air is moving faster than you are, and thus the force acts in the direction of travel. Swimming is also made possible by resistance: moving your palms and arms backwards creates a forward force (while the rest of your body is subject to a backward resistance force, making it harder to swim).

10 MAKE LIFTING EASIER

Simple machines (levers, pulleys, inclined planes, wedges) are used to reduce the effort needed to perform certain tasks, making them more convenient. Using a one-sided and a two-sided lever requires less force. The difference between the two types of levers lies in the location of their pivot points.

LESS WORK?

Does using simple machines mean doing less work hence saving energy?

Definitely not!

It would violate the law of conservation of energy. Less force (**F**) is exerted when simple machines are used, but this force acts "over a longer distance (**s**)", thus, the product of the two quantities does not change (**W = F · s**) – so the required work (**W**) is not reduced.

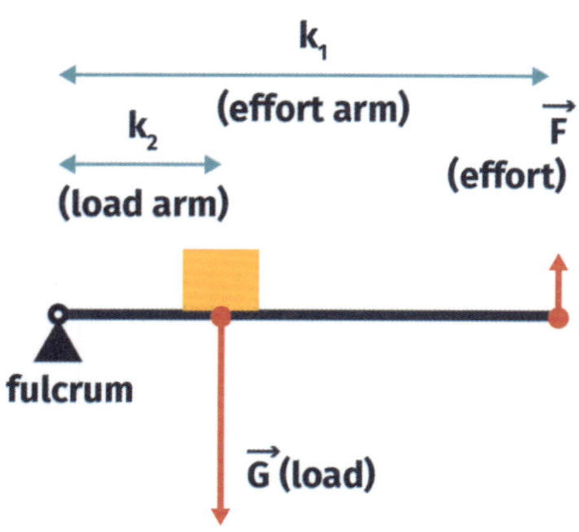

Balance of torques on one side

One-sided lever, but lifted with two hands

IF ONE-SIDED

A lever is a rigid body that can rotate around an axis, called the **fulcrum**. The load is the force exerted on the lever by the body to be lifted, and the distance from the line of action of the load to the axis of rotation is the **load arm**. The magnitude of the force required to lift is simply named lifting force. The **effort arm** is the distance from the line of action of the lifting force to the axis of rotation. If a rod is supported at its end and can therefore be rotated around its endpoint, it is a one-sided lever.

IF TWO-SIDED

If the bar is used in such a way that the fulcrum – and therefore the axis of rotation – is between the body to be lifted and the force we apply, it is a two-sided lever. The **equilibrium condition** for a lever means that the torques exerted by the two forces must be balanced (**$M_1 = M_2$**), i.e., the product of the lifting force and the effort arm must be equal to the product of the load and the load arm (**$F \cdot k_1 = G \cdot k_2$**).

IF THERE IS NO STOPPING

A wheel and axle is a two-sided lever consisting of two stationary pulleys mounted on a common axle, suitable for continuous lifting. The load is tied to the wheel with the smaller radius, while the lifting force is tied to the wheel with the larger radius, so that the force required to lift can be modified in proportion to the radius. The wheel is often replaced by a single crank. Examples are household grinders, spanners, or bicycle pedals.

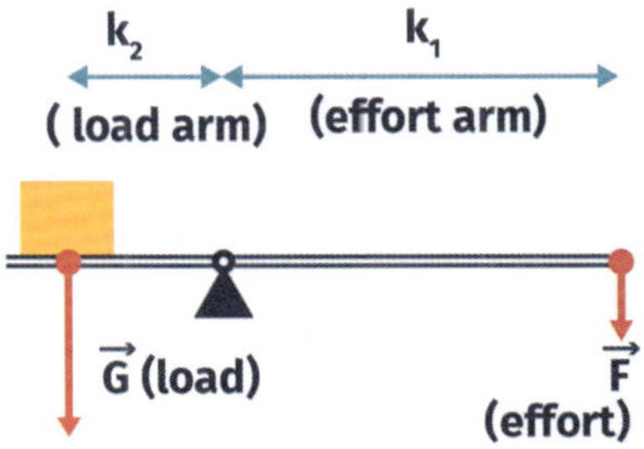

On one rod, but on two sides

The wheel, cylinder and crank

11 A PULLEY THAT WON'T BULLY

Although pulleys are simple machines operating on the same principle as levers, there is a big difference between them. While levers can only create a small amount of displacement, due to ropes (cables, chains), pulleys allow continuous lifting.

WHAT PULLEY?

A pulley is a disc with a groove around its circumference used to **lift a load** by using ropes. The pulley has a fixed axis. The load is lifted by means of a rope slung around the pulley. On construction sites, for example, the mortar bucket is lifted to the respective floor with the help of a fixed pulley.

Fixed pulley: the force is not reduced

IF YOU NEED TO LIFT A LOAD, BUT YOU ARE NOT STRONG ENOUGH

STATIONARY AND MOVABLE

In a **fixed pulley**, both the effort arm and the load arm are the radius of the pulley, so the force required to lift the load is equal to the weight of the load, but the direction of the force can be varied at will. Both the lifting force and the load pull the pulley in the same direction, so it is subjected to twice the load force. In the case of a **movable pulley**, the load is suspended on its axis of rotation. One end of the rope is fixed high and the other end is raised. One half of the load pulls on one end of the rope, the other half pulls on the other end. To lift the load, it is sufficient to exert half its weight, but twice the displacement is required.

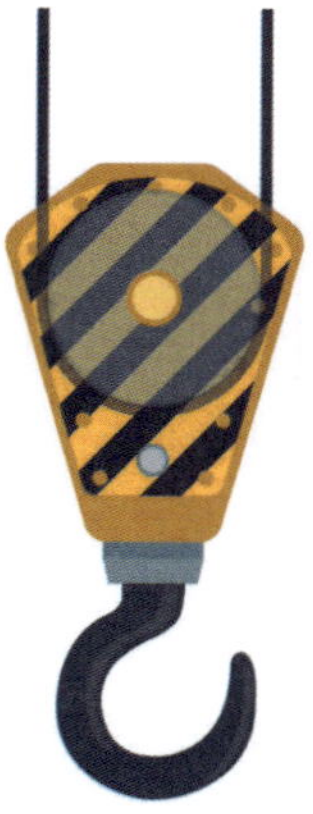

With half the force

SIMPLE

In practice, usually several stationary and movable pulleys are connected. The resulting system is called a compound pulley system. One type of this is the block and tackle, which consists of the same number of stationary and movable pulleys around which a single rope is slung. When used, the force required to lift the load uniformly is the **2n-th** part of the gravitational force acting on the load, where **n** is the number of movable pulleys in the pulley system: $F = G/2n$.

ARCHIMEDEAN

*Another special solution is the Archimedes pulley system, which consists of a stationary pulley and interconnected movable pulleys. Each movable pulley halves the force required to lift the load uniformly, so the force required to lift the load weight with a system of **n** pulleys can be calculated according to the following equation.*

$$F = \frac{m \cdot g}{2^n}$$

The work performed in this case is obviously not reduced either, so the required displacement of the rope is increased many times over.

An awesome solution

12 UP THE SLOPE

If we need to lift a heavy object, and neither a lever nor a pulley is available, the inclined plane, which itself is also a simple machine, can also be used for this purpose. The inclined plane has an angle to the horizontal and is suitable for sliding loads if the friction is not too great. Of course, it is useful not only for upward, but also for downward movements.

LET'S LIFT IT

When lifting, a vertical force must be applied which – assuming there is no acceleration – is equal to the weight of the body. The **gravitational force** (**G**) is the product of the mass of the **body** (**m**) and the **gravitational acceleration** (**g**): $G = m \cdot g$. If we are unable to apply the required force, or if we have to lift the object too far upwards, some help is needed.

$$g \approx 9.81 \frac{m}{s^2}$$

A serpentine road makes going uphill easier

Help is welcome

LESS WORK?

The work to be performed on the inclined plane is obviously not less than the work needed when lifting directly. The **force** decreases while the **distance travelled** (**s**) increases, so the increase in **potential energy** ($E_p = m \cdot g \cdot h$) at height **h** is equal to the work done on the inclined plane ($W = F \cdot s$). The longer the plane is, the smaller the angle of inclination to the horizontal, so a relatively smaller force is required for the work to be performed.

HOW BIG SHOULD THE INCLINATION BE?

If the body is moved upwards on an inclined plane, besides lifting the body, the friction **loss** should also be compensated by increasing our work. When designing the inclined plane, it is also important to take care so that it would neither be too long nor too short. On a longer slope, friction can significantly increase the amount of work required, even if the lifting force is lower.

Inclined planes for athletes

THE WEDGE AS AN INCLINED PLANE

A wedge is a special case of the inclined plane. It can be used for many purposes – for example, an axe has the same design. If we apply a great force on the wedge from above (hitting it), it penetrates the wood and transmits the thrust in both directions so that the wood can be split. The smaller the opening angle of the wedge is, the greater the lateral thrust is. The wedge is used in chisels, knife edges or even as a doorstop or to fasten machine parts. Wedges can also come in handy when parking on a sloping street, and we place them behind the wheels of our vehicle to prevent them from rolling away.

An axe and a wedge

13

LET'S COLLIDE

Collision is a momentary interaction between two bodies with large forces in action, which can even result in a deformation of the bodies. This can be considered with good approximation as a closed mechanical system where momentum is conserved. For simplicity's sake, only central collisions where the velocity vectors lie on the same line are discussed here.

"Numerous" collisions

INELASTIC

A collision between two bodies is completely inelastic when the bodies move together at the same velocity after the collision. If the law of conservation of momentum is applied here, the sum of the momenta before and after the collision is the same, i.e., $m_1 \cdot v_1 + m_2 \cdot v_2 = (m_1 + m_2) \cdot v_i$, from which the joint velocity can be derived:

$$v_i = \frac{m_1 \cdot v_1 + m_2 \cdot v_2}{m_1 + m_2}$$

When two cars with the same mass and the same velocity ($v_1 = v_2$) moving towards each other collide in a fully inelastic collision, they stop. The kinetic energy is reduced; in the meantime, deformation and heat are generated.

Moving towards each other

ELASTIC

In a perfectly elastic collision, the sum of the kinetic energy of the bodies involved is equal before and after the collision. The laws of conservation of momentum and energy also apply here. For bodies with the same mass, the velocities are reversed. **In reality, no fully elastic** collisions exist with rigid bodies.

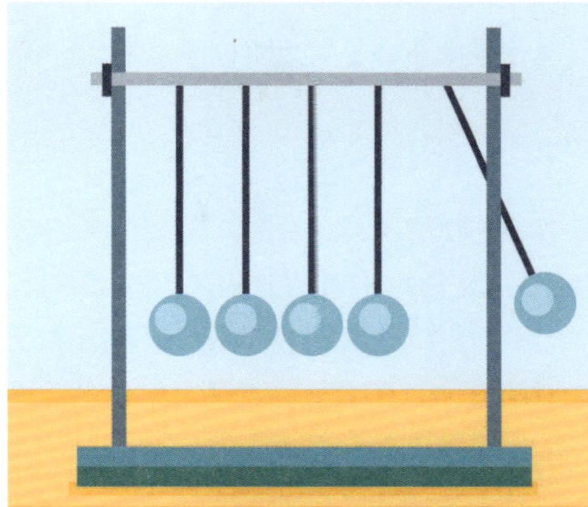

Newton's cradle: almost perfect

PLANNED

Vehicle designers must also consider how to minimise injuries to passengers in the event of a collision. **In a collision**, the passengers in the car are exposed to high accelerations (i.e., high forces). To minimise this, **crumple zones** are built into cars to make the impact as inelastic as possible. In a head-on-collision, the kinetic energy is absorbed by the crumple zone, thus protecting the passengers.

Crash test

14 RIDING WAVES

When the end of a taut rope is pulled up and down at right angles to the direction of the rope, a wave runs along the rope. If the experiment is repeated with a stretched spring pulled longitudinally, a different wave is produced.

MECHANICAL WAVES

A mechanical wave is a phenomenon in which an often **periodic disturbance** or deformation propagates in a system capable of oscillating (elastic medium) through the physical interaction of neighbouring particles in the medium.

The Mexican wave: the spectators move only upwards and downwards

GENERATION

A mechanical wave is transverse when the particles in the transmitting medium **move with a displacement perpendicular** to the direction of propagation. One example of this is the motion of a guitar string when hit. When the particles in the medium **move with a displacement parallel** to the direction of propagation, a longitudinal wave is created. The most typical example of this is the propagation of sound.

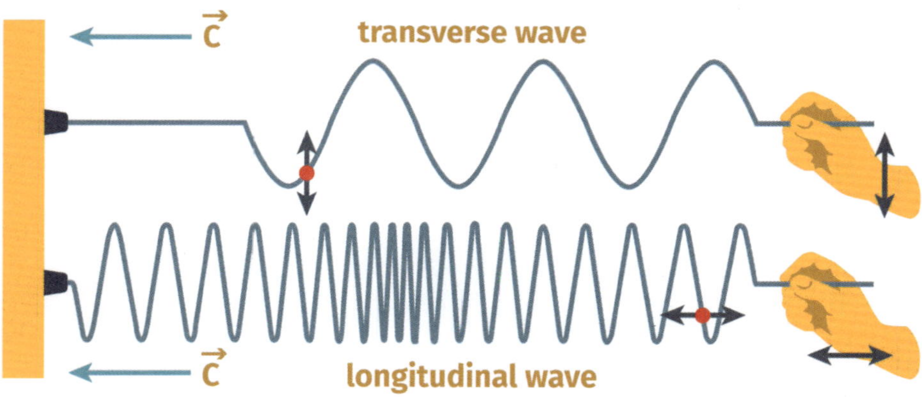

VIBRATING PROPAGATION

To describe wave motion, the physical properties introduced in the chapter about oscillatory motion are applied. The **period of a wave** (**T**) is the time required for the complete oscillatory motion of a particle. The reciprocal of this is the **frequency** (**f**), i.e., the number of oscillations that occur in one second. The distance between two neighbouring points moving in the same phase is the **wavelength** (**λ**), the maximum displacement of a point is the **amplitude** (**A**). The **velocity of propagation** (**c**) is the ratio of the wavelength to the period. It describes the velocity of the wave movement and can also be defined using frequency.

$$c=\frac{\lambda}{T}$$

$$c=\lambda\cdot f$$

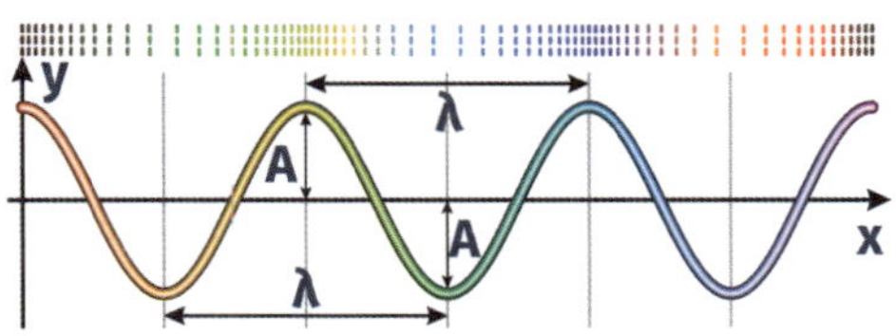

Characteristics

AT THE FRONTLINE

In a ripple tank, external action on the water surface creates plane waves, the higher parts of which are called wave crests and the lower parts are called wave troughs. The waves generated by the end of a thin stick are circular waves extending outwards from the point of the stick as the centre. Successive wave fronts move outwards in a ring. However, if the edge of a ruler is used to set the particles along the ruler in motion simultaneously, the successive wave fronts will be parallel to the edge of the ruler.

15 REFRACTION / REFLECTION

When a mechanical wave propagates, it often happens that the wave travels in one medium and arrives at another one. Depending on the type of the wave and the materials of the two media, several events may occur. The wave often changes direction or is partially reflected at the boundary of the new medium. However, the wave may also be completely reflected from the new medium.

THE LIGHT

The propagation of light is also a wave phenomenon. When we pour water into a transparent glass, the spoon placed in it appears to be broken at the boundary between the air and the water when viewed from most angles. Placing the glass on a glass table, the objects inside appear upside down.

Peculiarities

DIFFERENT ELSEWHERE

The explanation offered by the discipline of materials science for this is the following: neighbouring particles being more closely bound together can transmit the phases of vibrational states faster. If you **compare two media**, the one in which the waves propagate faster is the denser one in terms of wave transmission.

BROKEN

If the **boundary surface** between the two media is not perpendicular to the direction of the wave propagation, the direction of movement of the wave also changes, i.e., the wave is refracted. In this case, the sines of the angle of incidence **α** and the angle of refraction **β** at the boundary of the two media are in the same proportion to each other as the propagation velocities (**c_1** and **c_2**) for the respective media. From this law it follows that when entering (not perpendicularly) a medium with greater density, the angle of refraction is smaller, while when entering a medium with the smaller density, it is larger than the angle of incidence.

$$\frac{\sin\alpha}{\sin\beta} = \frac{c_1}{c_2}$$

REFLECTED

The quotient of the velocities $\mathbf{c_1/c_2}$ *in the two media is the relative refractive index of the second medium with respect to the first, denoted by* $\mathbf{n_{2,1}}$*. When the wave reaches a medium with lower density, the angle of refraction will exceed the angle of incidence. When the angle of incidence is increased, the angle of refraction reaches 90° at one point. The corresponding angle of incidence is the critical angle of total reflection. If the angle of incidence exceeds this value, total reflection occurs, and the wave does not penetrate the other medium.*

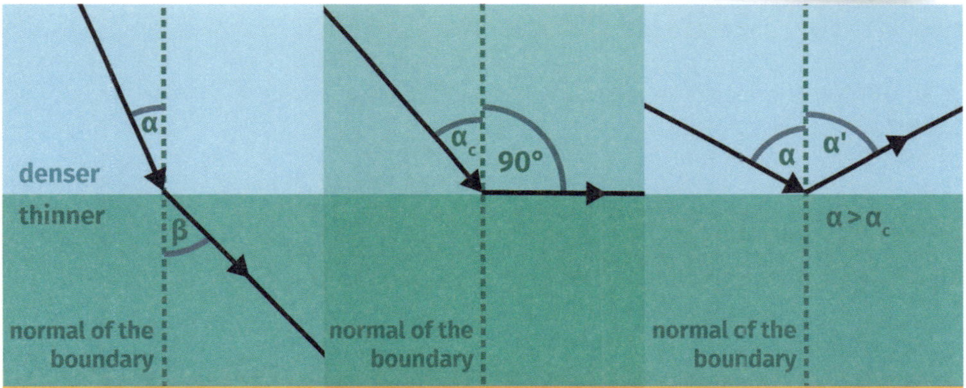

Refraction where ß > α | *Refraction where* α_c *is the critical angle of total reflection* | *Total reflection where α = α'*

16

STANDING WAVES

Standing waves (special cases of interference) occur when waves with the same frequency and amplitude interact with each other.

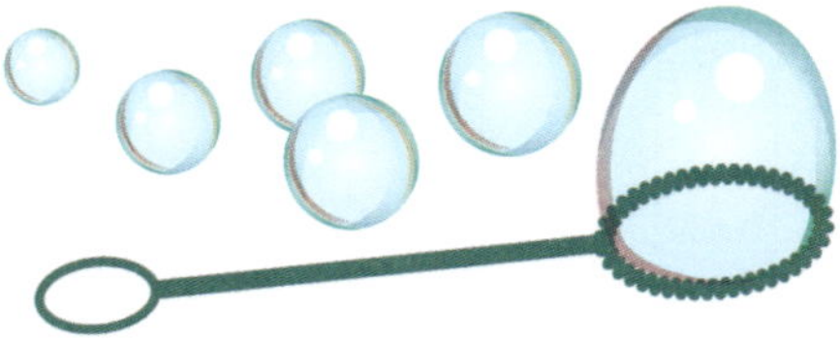

FORMATION

A standing wave is often created when a wave is reflected at the boundary of a medium, i.e., it is created by the **interference of the incoming wave and the reflected wave**. Let's fix the end of a long rubber band and vibrate its other end slowly at first, then with increasing speed. We can observe that at certain frequencies standing waves are created on the band, i.e., some points of the band are stationary (nodes), while others have maximal displacement (anti-nodes).

NODES

Each point of the band oscillates with a **position-dependent amplitude**, between two nodes the points are in phase, on the two sides of the node they are in the opposite phase. The distance between two adjacent wave nodes is half the full wavelength (**$\lambda/2$**), and this also applies to two adjacent anti-nodes. As the frequency increases, the number of nodes increases, so the wavelength decreases.

Battle rope: creating waves can also make you fit

With variable frequency

ON THE SURFACE

Standing waves are not only generated on elastic bands, which are considered one-dimensional, but also on flat or curved surfaces. The nodes that separate the anti-nodes form **stationary nodal lines**. A simple **standing wave on a surface** can also be created with a soap bubble-blowing stick. If you move the stick at the right frequency, half of a standing wave forms at the surface of the bubble, with the anti-node in the middle, and a circular nodal line at the edges.

Half wave on a bubble

MUSICAL

The guitar string is flexible, so the deformation caused by plucking spreads out and is reflected at the ends, creating a standing wave. The vibrating string produces the sound: the more it vibrates, the stronger the sound is. The shorter the strings, the higher the sound, but the frequency can also be changed by tensioning the strings: this is called tuning. A less taut string sounds lower, while a tighter one higher. When the string is plucked, several notes sound at once, the resultant of them is the timbre.

17 MIND THE GAP!

Let's create plane waves in a ripple tank and put an obstacle with a changeable gap in the way. It can be observed that with continuous reduction of the gap, the wave phenomenon extends to the entire region of the geometric shadow. When bent (diffracted), the wave enters the space behind an obstacle located in the direction of propagation, and in the process both its direction and properties are changed.

HOW DOES IT WORK?

A theoretical explanation of the fundamental laws of wave propagation was formulated by **Christiaan Huygens**, a Dutch mathematician, physicist, and astronomer, in 1678. However, Huygens' principle cannot explain the phenomenon of diffraction. To explain diffraction, the French physicist **Augustin-Jean Fresnel** developed an extension of Huygens' principle in 1819. According to Huygens' principle, the points of a given wave front can be regarded as sources of circular elementary waves (spherical waves in space). The enveloping curve (enveloping surface) of the circular waves (spherical waves) emanating from these elementary wave sources results in the subsequent wave front. With the help of Huygens' principle, the behaviour of the wave at the interface of two media can be explained, i.e., the refraction and reflection of the wave.

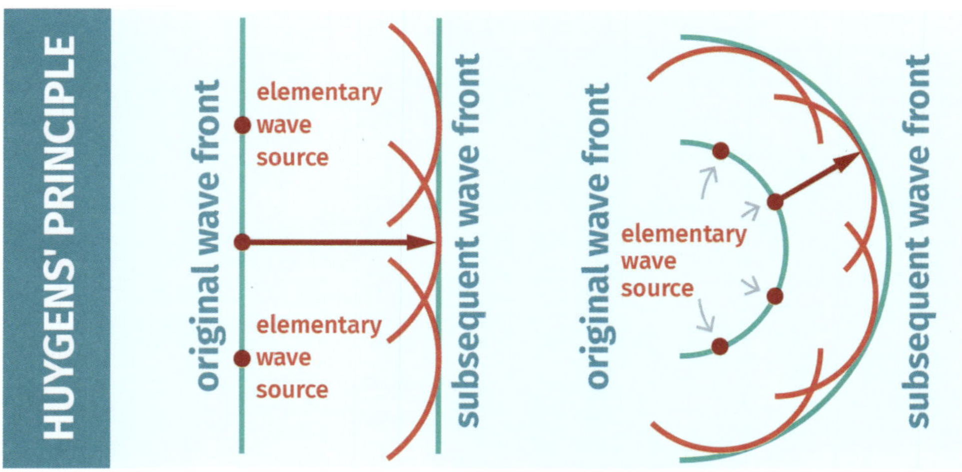

Wave fronts for plane and circular waves

THE EXTENSION

The **Huygens-Fresnel principle** states that each point in the wave field behaves like a source of elementary waves. The phenomena observed in the wave field are produced by the interference of these elementary waves. When the wave passes through a gap, an interference pattern appears behind the gap that corresponds to the interference of coherent waves, the source of which are an infinite number of imaginary elementary wave sources located in the gap.

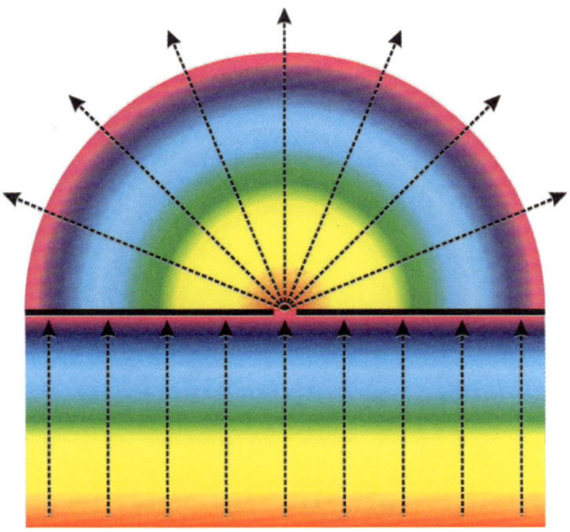

Through wide and narrow gaps

FRESNEL LENS

Also, it was Fresnel who developed the stepped collector lens – bearing his name –, and through which the transmitted light rays continue in parallel. A device built with this lens is much lighter and also smaller. Originally developed for lighthouses, the lens is now used in car headlights, projectors, and cameras.

LED lamp with Fresnel lens

18

POLARISATION

Let's induce transverse waves on a flexible rope, and let's change the plane of oscillation continuously. If we pass the rope through a narrow vertical slit, we can see that the points of the rope behind the slit vibrate only in the vertical plane. If the rope is then passed through another slit, a horizontal one this time, the wave phenomenon disappears completely.

CIRCULAR OR ELLIPTICAL

A linearly polarised wave oscillates in a plane, however, there are other types of polarisation. The **special case** in which every point of the transverse wave performs a uniform circular motion perpendicular to the direction of propagation is called a circularly polarised wave. In addition, there is the elliptically polarised wave, whose motion follows an elliptical orbit.

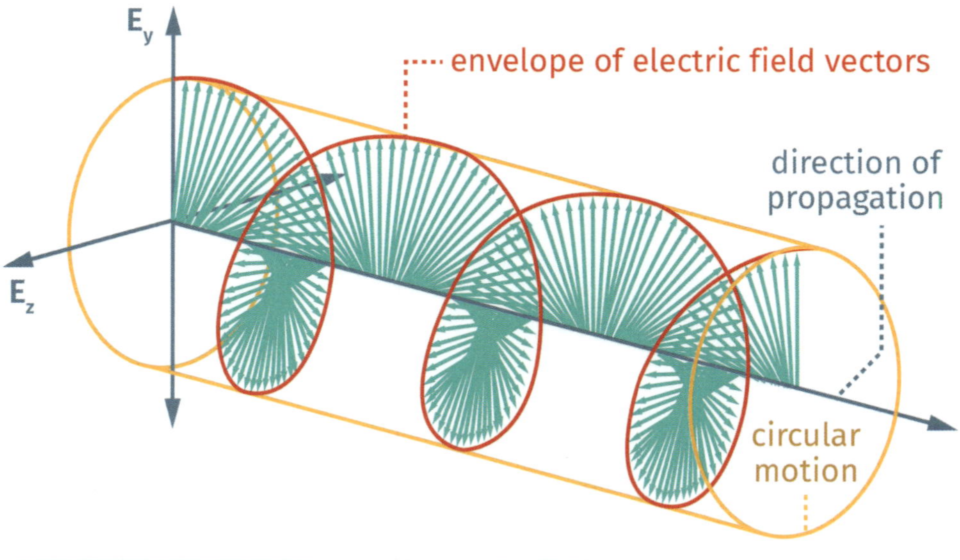

Circularly polarised electromagnetic wave

THE WAVES

The polarised wave can be separated from the "mixed" (unpolarised) wave by the polariser, which only allows a transverse wave of a certain direction to pass through a thin gap. If the polarised wave is allowed to pass through a gap (analyser) perpendicular to the plane of vibration, the vibration terminates. If the analyser is placed parallel to the plane of oscillation, the wave travels on. In case of a longitudinal wave, the direction of propagation is the same as the direction of oscillation, so the wave travels through the gap undisturbed.

Effect of the polariser

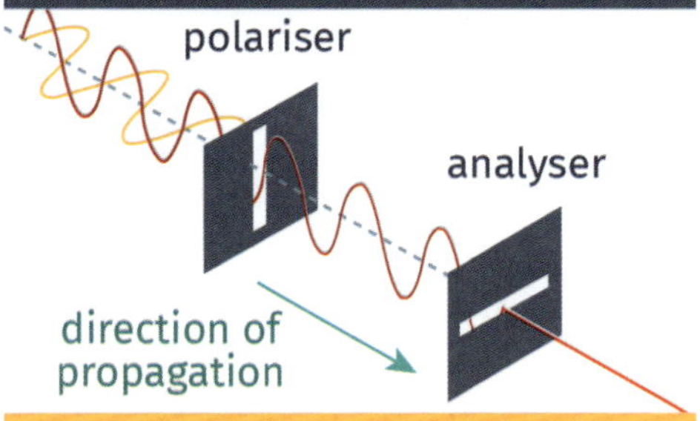

Termination of the wave phenomenon through two perpendicular gaps

THE LIGHT

In longitudinal waves, such as sound waves, particles vibrate parallel to the direction of propagation of the wave. They cannot be polarised. Light, on the other hand, is an **electromagnetic wave** in which the electric and magnetic waves are perpendicular to each other and also to the direction of propagation. A polariser for light is a special light-refracting material used in sunglasses or in photography as a filter to reduce mirror effects.

3D

Our spatial perception ability is based on the fact that our two eyes see slightly different images, from which it is the brain that "produce" a spatial image. 3D televisions and cinemas achieve the spatial effect through special glasses, the two lenses of which allow light with different polarisation to pass through.

19 MIRROR, MIRROR ON THE WALL...

We see the image of an object when a diverging beam of light, seemingly emanating from a single point, enters our eyes. We see it at the exact point where the rays of light that reach our eyes appear to originate. If the light rays from the object enter our eyes without changing direction, we see the actual object directly; if they are previously reflected, refracted, or passed through an optical device, we only see the image of the object.

IMAGE FROM RAYS

In **optical imaging**, divergent light rays emanating from a point of an object (**O**) are brought back together by means of an optical device to produce the image of the object point (**I**). The **real image** can be projected onto a screen, but since the beam of light leaving the imaging device during the imaging process is divergent, a **virtual image** appears as the extension of the rays.

The object and the image are symmetrical to the plane of the mirror

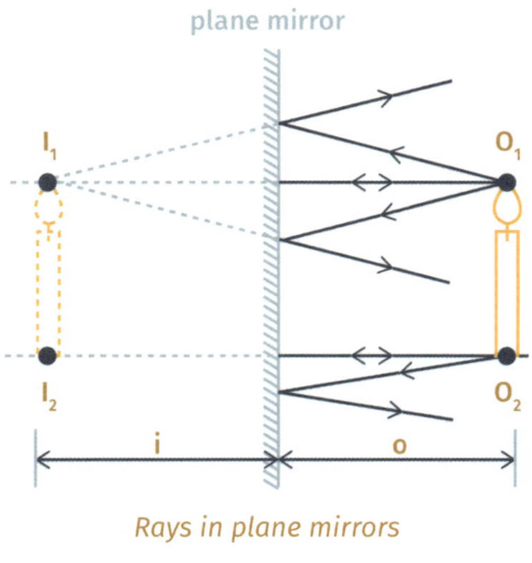

Rays in plane mirrors

ON A FLAT SURFACE

A beam of light is reflected from the surface of a plane mirror **at the same angle** as the angle of incidence. During imaging, a virtual image is formed on the other side of the mirror surface, at the same distance as the object, along the extension of the light rays, i.e., $|i|=o$. The imaging of the plane mirror projects the object points O_1 and O_2 into the image points I_1 and I_2 just as it brings any other point of the object **O** into the corresponding point of the image **I**.

ON THE OUTER SURFACE OF A SPHERE

A convex spherical mirror scatters parallel rays of light in such a way that the extensions of the rays appear to emanate from a single point. This point is called the **focal point** (**F**), and its distance from the optical centre of the mirror is called the **focal length** (**f**), which has a negative sign for convex mirrors. The resulting image is virtual, has the same orientation, and is reduced in size because it is formed behind the mirror. The law of imaging, which describes the connection between object distance, image distance and focal length, also applies to convex spherical mirrors.

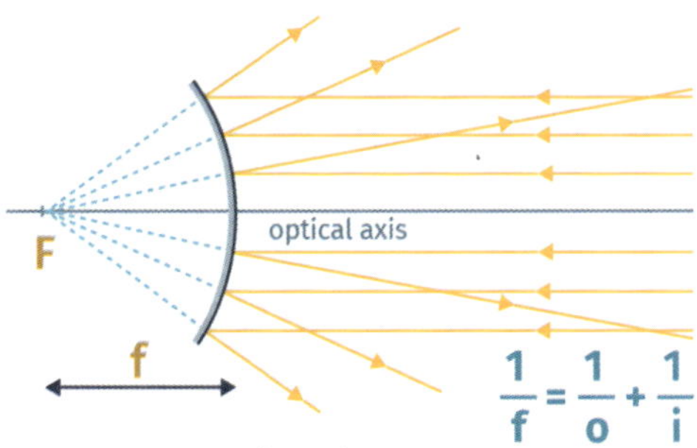

Diverging rays

IN TRAFFIC

Another special optical path of the convex spherical mirror is where the rays directed at the focal point are reflected parallel to the optical axis. Convex mirrors are widely used in traffic, – for example, as rear-view mirrors in cars – because they significantly magnify the field of view. However, we should not forget that everything appears smaller in them!

A PLANE MIRROR IS A SPHERICAL MIRROR WITH AN INFINITE RADIUS

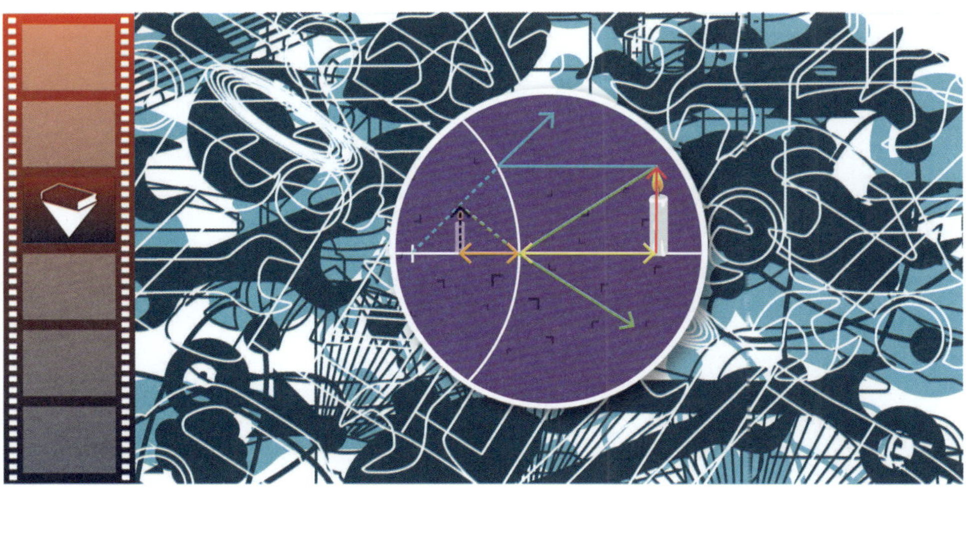

20

IN THE CONCAVE MIRROR

A concave spherical mirror is a mirror with a small aperture angle coated with a light-reflecting layer on its curved inner surface. Light rays from its reflective surface are reflected converging so that light rays from a point on an object at a suitable distance are collected into a single point. When a screen is placed at this point, the image becomes visible, i.e., a real image is formed.

APPLICATIONS

A concave spherical mirror is used by the dentist to examine the areas inside the mouth that are difficult to see. The reason for this is that this mirror provides a magnified image from a certain distance. Due to the feature that it collects rays, otolaryngologists use a mirror placed on the forehead, which enables the doctor to see dark areas better through the hole in the centre of the mirror.

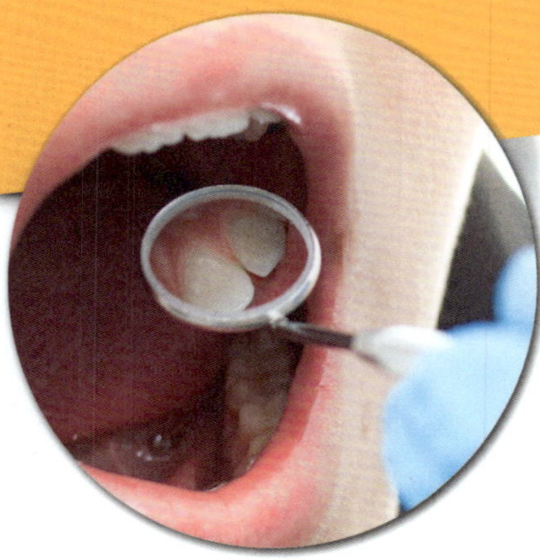

LIGHT BEAMS

An important concept of the concave spherical mirror is the **optical axis**, which passes through the **geometric centre** (**G**) of the spherical surface and divides the mirror into two halves. The **optical centre** (**C**) is the point of intersection between this axis and the mirror. The most important optical paths include rays that run parallel to the optical axis and pass through the **focal point** (**F**) after reflection. Light rays passing through the focal point are reflected parallel to the optical axis, while the light rays that pass through the optical centre follow a path symmetrical to the optical axis, and the ones that pass through the geometric centre are reflected into themselves.

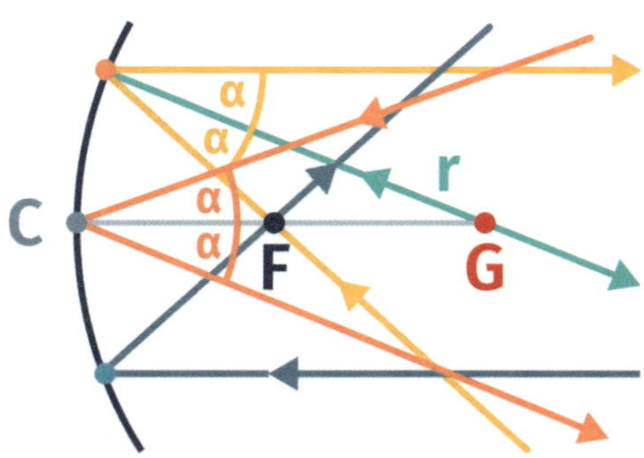

The most important optical paths

IMAGES

Imaging is influenced by the **object distance** (**o**): if it is smaller than the **focal length** (**f**), a magnified, upright, virtual image is produced. If it is between one and two times the focal length, a magnified, inverted, real image is produced. If it is greater than twice the focal length, a reduced, inverted, and real image is produced. If the object distance and the focal length are identical, no image is produced.

EVEN MORE RAYS

The concave spherical mirror can also be used to reflect electromagnetic waves with wavelengths other than visible light. The commonly known satellite dish also contains a large concave mirror that converges the signals from the satellites into a receiving antenna placed at the focal point.

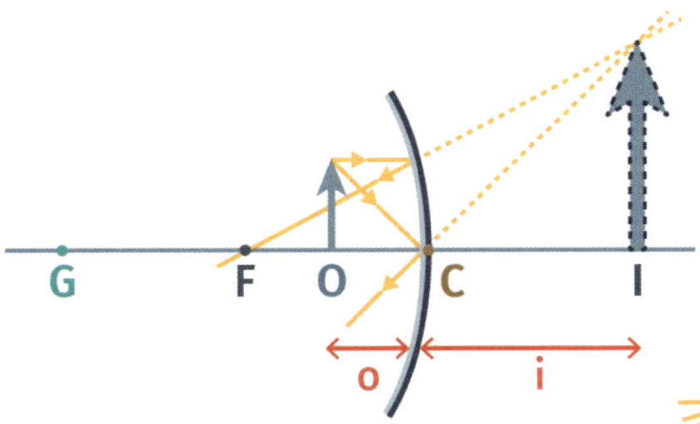

Inside the focal point

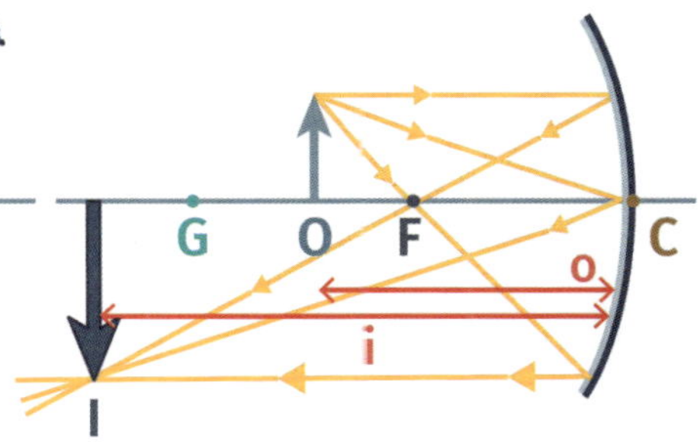

Outside the focal point

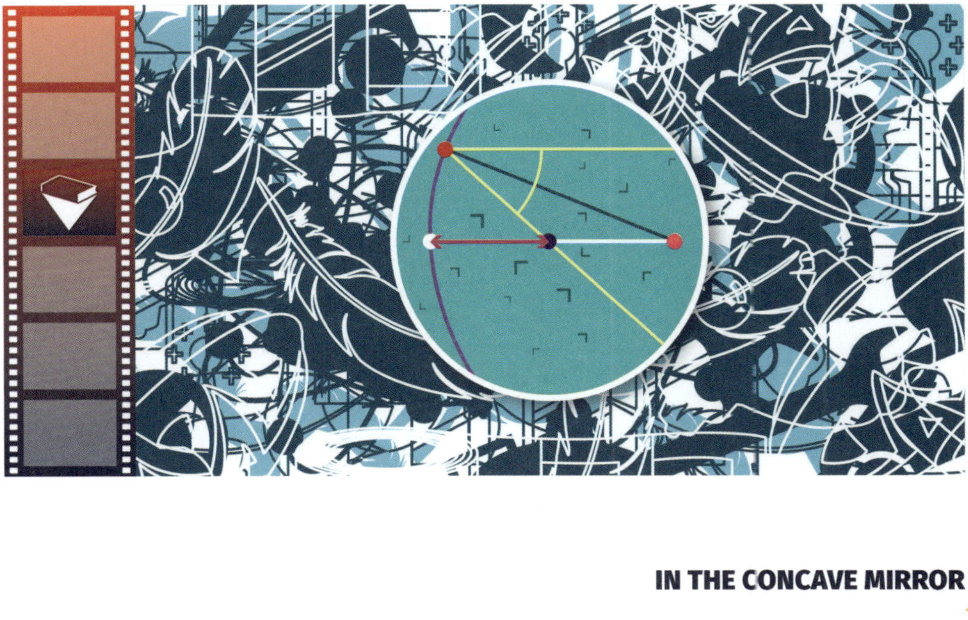

21 LET'S REFRACT THE LIGHT

Light often plays tricks on us by passing through different media, creating optical illusions. We encounter the phenomenon of light passing through a pane of glass every day: the images that appear through the window glass are not exactly where we see them.

THE LAW

Air and glass are of different densities, which makes light waves travel at different speeds when travelling through them. As they pass from one to the other, their direction is also changed. The refractive index of the second medium with respect to the first medium is the ratio of the sines of the angle of incidence and the angle of refraction, this is called ***Snell's law****.*

Sides of glass panes

PLANE-PARALLEL PLATE

An **optically refractive medium** – i.e., a transparent body – **with parallel plane outer surfaces** is called a plane-parallel plate. Let us direct a beam of light onto a glass plate with thickness **d** and refractive index **n** (where $n = c_{air} / c_{glass}$). We can see that after two refractions the light beam continues to be parallel to the original direction, but it is slightly shifted to the side. The size of the shift (**Δx**) depends on the thickness of the plate, its refractive index, and the angle of incidence. It is this shift that causes the small difference between the position of the image observed and the actual one.

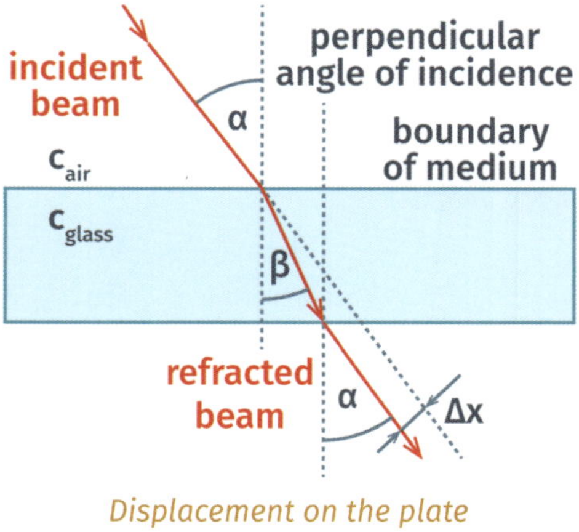

Displacement on the plate

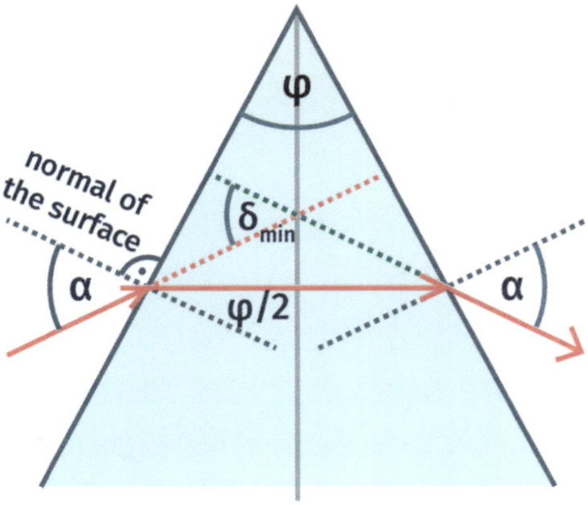

Refraction of light on the two planes

PRISM

An **optically refractive medium** (transparent body) **with plane outer surfaces at an angle to each other** is called a prism. The prism usually has a triangular base; the angle subtended by the two planes is called the prism angle. The light that falls on a prism is refracted both when it enters and when it leaves the prism. The extent of double refraction (**δ**) depends on the refractive index, the angle of incidence of the light (**α**), and the prism angle (**φ**).

DECOMPOSITION OF LIGHT

When white light falls on a prism, it is refracted both as it enters and as it leaves. When we carry out this experiment, we will also notice that the outgoing beam of light is no longer white but shows the entire spectrum of colours. White light is a **composite light** that is refracted differently at different wavelengths due to the phenomenon of **dispersion**.

Colours are created from white light

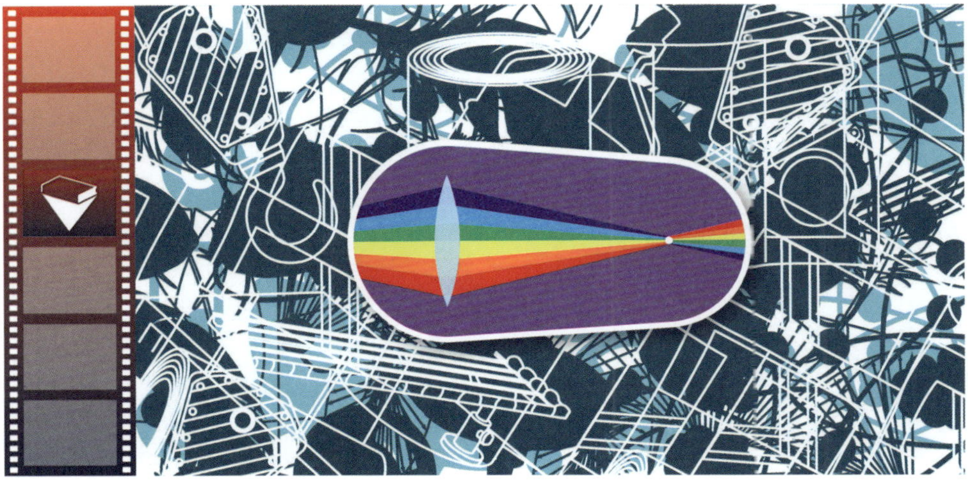

22

COLLECTING LIGHT

An optical lens is a transparent body that usually has two spherical outer surfaces, or in some cases one plane and one spherical outer surface. Its optical behaviour is not only determined by the shape of the lens, but the material also plays a role in whether the lens collects or disperses the light rays. From an optical point of view, we thus speak of converging lenses and diverging lenses.

CONVEX

A convex lens collects the light rays that run parallel to the optical axis in one point – the focal point – and is therefore also called a converging lens. Depending on the design of the two sides, a distinction is made between lenses with concave and convex outer surfaces, i.e., concave-convex lenses, with flat and convex surfaces, i.e., plano-convex lenses, and bi-convex lenses, which are convex on both sides.

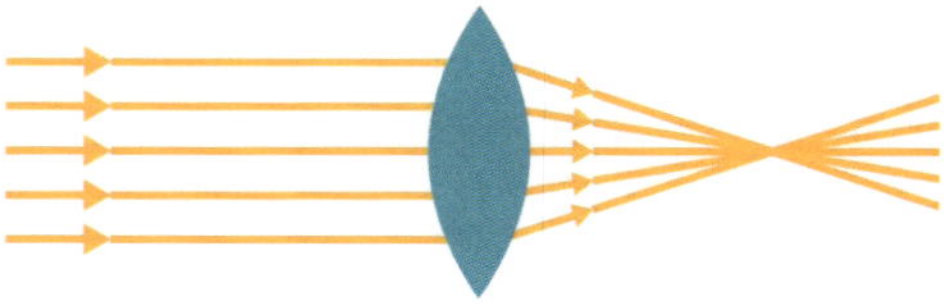

Bi-convex lens

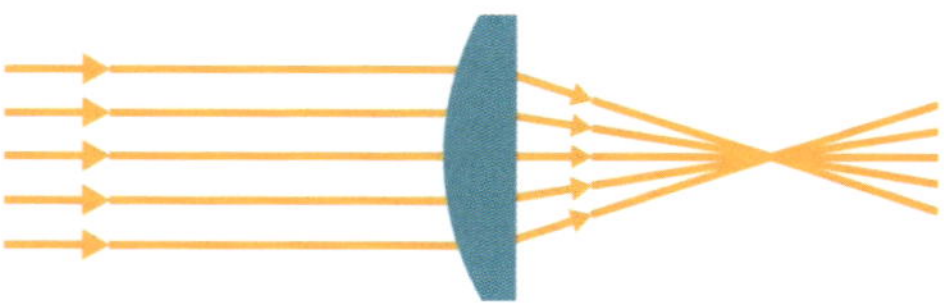

Plano-convex lens

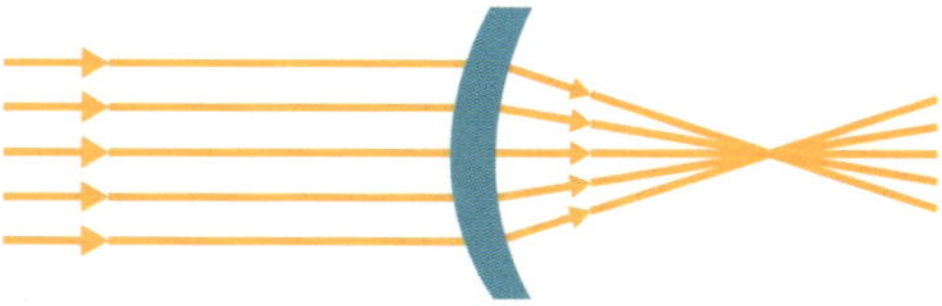

Concave-convex lens

TYPICALLY

In optical systems, **typical optical paths** are defined in order to be able to outline the resulting image. In the case of a convex lens, these include the beam parallel to the optical axis that passes through the focal point after refraction, the beam passing through the focal point that continues parallel to the optical axis after refraction, and the beam directed towards the centre of the lens that continues without refraction.

The focal point can get hot

IMAGING

The following figure depicts images of objects of the same size in the most important positions. The typical optical paths of imaging are used to outline the image. If the object is outside the double focal length, i.e., **2f < o** (yellow arrow), a reduced, inverted, real image is produced. If **2f = o** (green arrow), image and object have the same size. If **f < o < 2f** (red arrow), an enlarged, inverted, real image is produced.

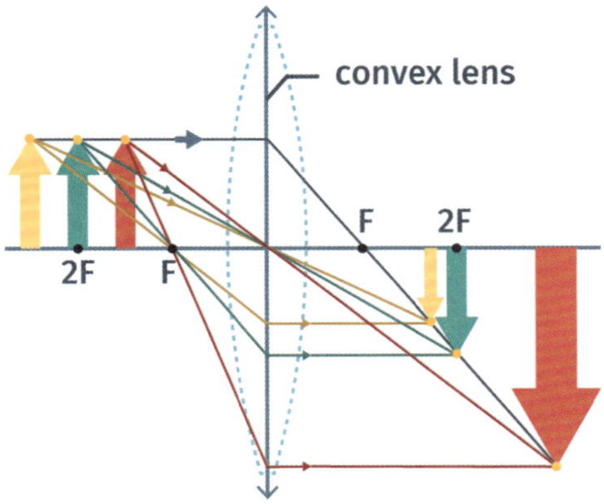

The object and its images

LET'S USE IT

Magnifying glasses and loupes are simple convex lenses used for viewing details of objects with some magnification. For the far-sighted, glasses with convex lenses are also prescribed to see closer objects and letters better. An important piece of equipment in biology – the microscope – also has a convex lens, but it can also be an important part of telescopes. With these tools, we can examine target objects at a significant angular magnification.

A magnifying glass, or is it a loupe?

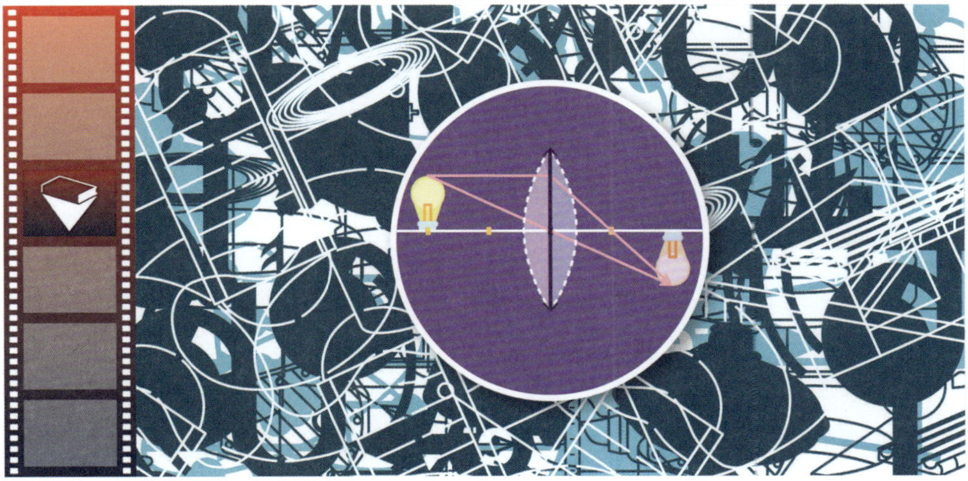

23

DIVERGING LENSES

A concave lens scatters the light rays running parallel to the optical axis in a way that their backward extensions meet at a single point, namely at the focal point. Because the beam of light passing through the lens diverges, a concave lens is also called a diverging lens. Optical lenses, including the concave lens, can be modelled using multiple prisms with varying angles.

CONCAVELY

The concave lens is constructed in such a way that **it is always thinner in the centre than at the edges**. This can be achieved in various ways, but one side of the lens is always concave. Based on the design of the other side, a distinction is made between lenses with a double concave or bi-concave surface, with a flat, or plano-concave surface, and with a convex, or convex-concave surface.

Bi-concave lens

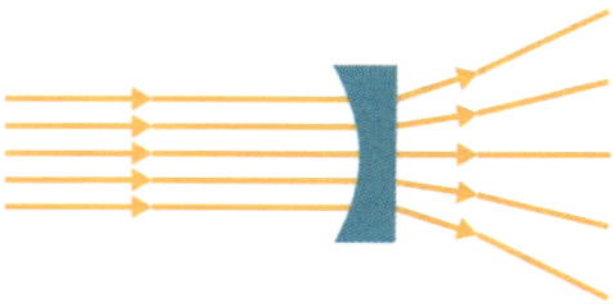

Plano-concave lens

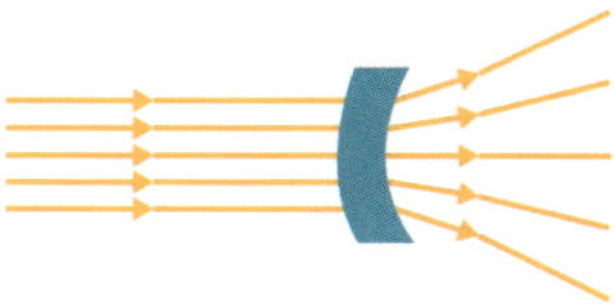

Convex-concave lens

RAY PATHS

The optical paths that can be used to outline the path of a ray of light for the concave lens: **1.** A ray of light parallel to the optical axis, the backward extension of which – after refraction – passes through the focal point on the arrival side of the lens. **2.** A ray of light travelling in the direction of the focal point behind the lens, which – after refraction – continues parallel to the optical axis. **3.** A ray directed towards the centre of the lens, which continues without refraction.

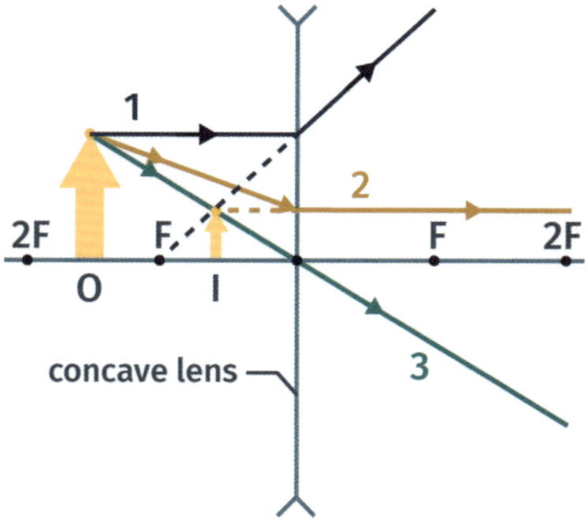

Outlining the image of the object

FORMATION OF AN IMAGE

After the outlining is carried out, it can be seen that the resulting image is always virtual, reduced and upright, regardless of the position of the object. The **thin lens equation**, i.e., the equation establishing a close link between the object distance, image distance and focal length, also confirms this.

$$\frac{1}{f}=\frac{1}{o}+\frac{1}{i}$$

The focal length of concave lenses is negative, so it can be seen that for any given object distance, based on the magnification value (**M**), we will always get a reduced image.

$$M=\frac{i}{o}=\frac{f}{o-f}$$

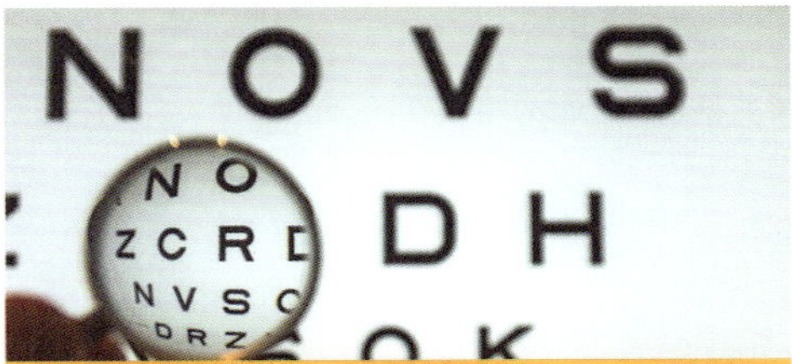

Reduced

LET'S TAKE A CLOSER LOOK

For short-sighted people, we use concave lenses to prevent light rays from distant objects to be focused too close. If we look closely at the design of the lens, we will see that convex-concave lenses, rather than bi-concave lenses, are used in glasses and contact lenses.

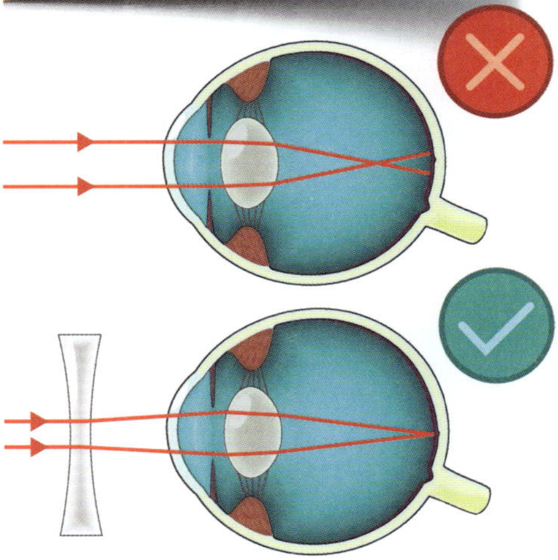

Perfect vision even at a distance

24 DISTANT EXAMINATIONS

Images of small, close objects can be magnified with a microscope or a magnifying lens. To observe distant objects, telescopes are used. The objects in this case are so far away that the light rays emanating from them are essentially parallel. The telescope's optical system is used to increase the viewing angle of the objects under examination.

WITH LENSES

The first telescope used for astronomical purposes was built by Galileo Galilei. His telescope, presented in 1609, consisted of a convex lens and a concave lens. The converging lens with a large cross-section focused the parallel rays, which were then parallelised again by a concave lens before the focal point, so that the observer's eye receives much more light from the observed object, under a much larger viewing angle, than without the telescope.

Refracting telescope (refractor) using lenses

WHEN IT HAS TO BE BIGGER

Making larger convex lenses would be very expensive, thus objects in the distance like far away galaxy clusters are usually observed with **reflecting telescopes** containing mirrors. Instead of a converging lens, the light rays are focused by a concave mirror, which is cheaper to produce, and it creates an inverted image. Further transformation of the image requires a mirror and lens system.

Reflecting telescope (reflector) using mirrors

THE STARS IN VIEW

Telescopes with the highest magnifications are used in observatories. An **observatory** is a special building erected at a great height. The central element is the telescope, which can not only be moved upwards and downwards, but with the right mechanism can also be rotated to follow the movement of the stars.

Observatory

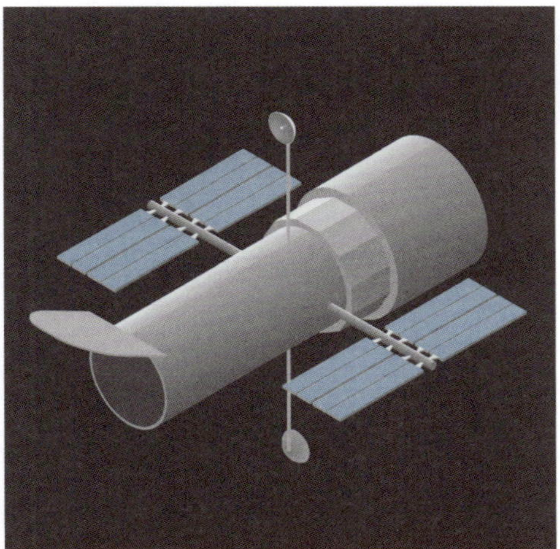

The Hubble Space Telescope

WHEN IT HAS TO BE EVEN BIGGER

The larger the cross-section of the tube, the better the telescope, because it can collect more light. The largest telescopes have a mirror diameter of almost 10 metres. It is quite challenging to create even larger mirrors. More recently, the performance of telescopes has been improved by the use of **coordinated telescope systems**. Atmospheric turbulences can be eliminated by using space telescopes, observing from above the atmosphere.

25

THE ELECTRIC FIELD

An electrically charged body is with the property that it is surrounded by an electric field. The electric field exerts a force on a charged body placed in it. At each point, the properties of the electric field can be investigated using a small test charge that is considered point-like.

PROPERTIES

If a test charge **q** is placed in a particular point of an electric field and thus subjected to a force **F**, the ratio of the force and the charge can be used to describe the strength of the field. This ratio is called electric field **E**, which is a vector quantity. Its direction corresponds to the direction of the force acting on the positive test charge, and has the unit **N/C**, or more commonly **V/m**.

$$E=\frac{F}{q}$$

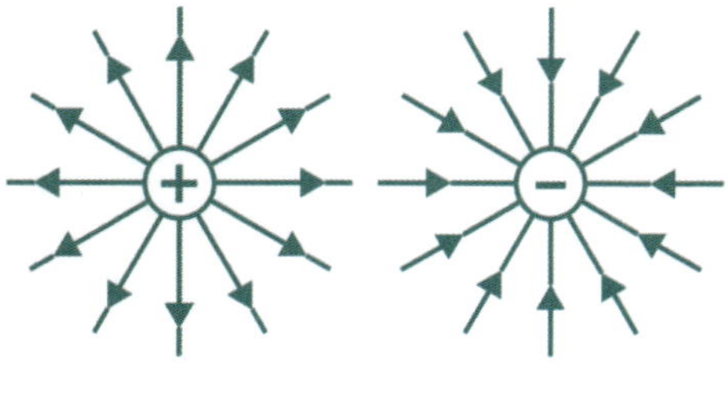

Electric field lines of point-like charges

STRENGTH

Let's calculate the electric field of a point charge **Q**. Let us place a test charge **q** at a distance **r** from it. The magnitude of the force **F** acting between them is determined by Coulomb's law (where the value of the **k** Coulomb constant is approx. $9\cdot10^9\,Nm^2/C^2$):

$$F=k\cdot\frac{q\cdot Q}{r^2}$$

The magnitude of the electric field is derived from this:

$$E=\frac{F}{q}=k\cdot\frac{Q}{r^2}$$

The electric field is radial in every point, its direction is given by the sign of the charge **Q**. In case of a positive charge the vectors of the field point in the direction which is opposite to the direction of the charge ("outwards") while in case of a negative charge they point in the direction of the charge ("inwards").

THE LINES

Field lines are imaginary curves with a positive charge at their origin and a negative charge at their end, the tangent at each point being the **vector of the electric field**. A single field line passes through each point. The field lines must be plotted in a way that their number (density) is proportional to the electric field. A point-like charge creates an inhomogeneous electric field. Where an electric field is homogeneous, the field lines have the same direction and density everywhere.

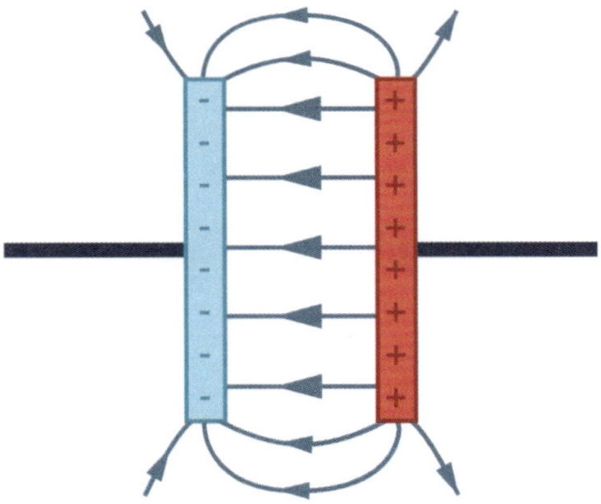

Homogeneous electric field between the plates

SUPERPOSITION

*If several forces act simultaneously on a point charge, the superposition principle applies, i.e., the resulting force acting on a given point charge is the vector sum of the calculated forces. In the following picture, we place a positive charge **q** at a point of the electric field generated by two charges. Since it is closer to the positive charge **Q**, the repulsive force is the greater one, and the vector of the net force lies at the tangent of the field line passing through this point.*

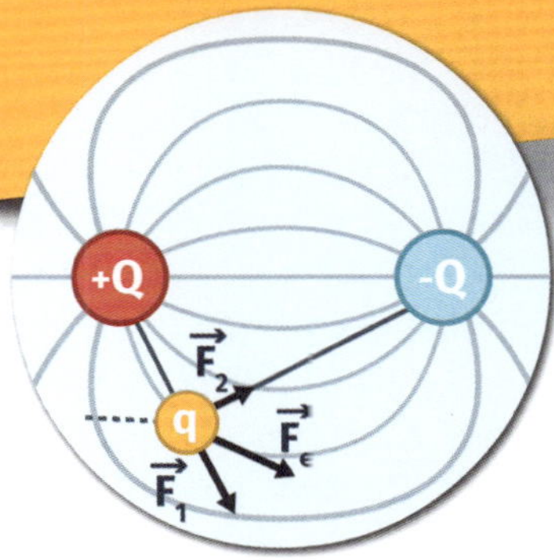

Derivation of the net force

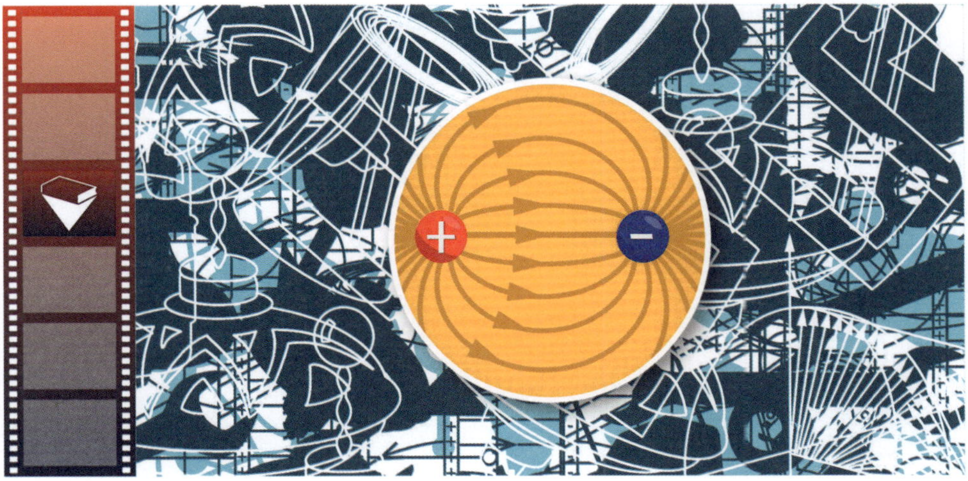

26 WORK AND VOLTAGE

An electric field exerts a force $F = E \cdot q$ on a test object with a charge q placed in it, which can move electrically charged objects or can hinder their movement. Therefore, like gravity, the electric field can perform work.

IN WHICH DIRECTION DOES IT MOVE?

If the displacement **s** of a positive charge **q** in an electric field is parallel to and in the same direction as the field lines, the work performed by the field is $\mathbf{W_1 = F \cdot s = E \cdot Q \cdot s}$. For a displacement of the same magnitude in the opposite direction, the work is negative, i.e., the mover of the charge performs the work against the field: $\mathbf{W_2 = -W_1}$. However, if the displacement vector s is perpendicular to the field lines, the dot product of their vectors is zero, i.e., in this case no work is performed: $\mathbf{W_3 = W_4 = 0}$.

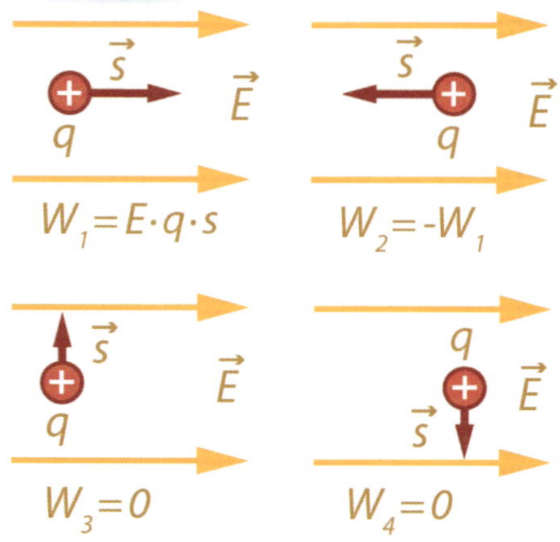

Charge in the electric field

PERFORMING WORK

When a charge **Q** is moved from a given point **A** to a point **B** in an electric field generated by stationary charges, the work performed does not depend on the path of the movement, but only on the position of points **A** and **B**. This constant is the voltage of point **A** relative to point **B** and is denoted by $\mathbf{U_{AB}}$. The unit of voltage is the volt, its symbol is **V**. The voltage between two points in an electric field is **1V** if **1C** charge requires **1J** of work to be moved from one point to the other.

$$\frac{W_{AB}}{Q} = \text{constant}$$

$$U_{AB} = \frac{W_{AB}}{Q}$$

ROUND AND ROUND

In a homogeneous field, if the displacement is in the direction of the electric field, the voltage is the product of the electric field and the displacement.

$$U_{AB} = \frac{W_{AB}}{Q} = \frac{E \cdot Q \cdot s}{Q} = E \cdot s$$

Subsequently, if the charge is brought back from point **B** to point **A**, $W_{BA} = -W_{AB}$, and therefore $U_{BA} = -U_{AB}$. If the start and end points of the movement are the same, i.e., along a closed curve, the total work performed on the charge **Q** is zero, in other words, the voltage in a closed loop is zero.

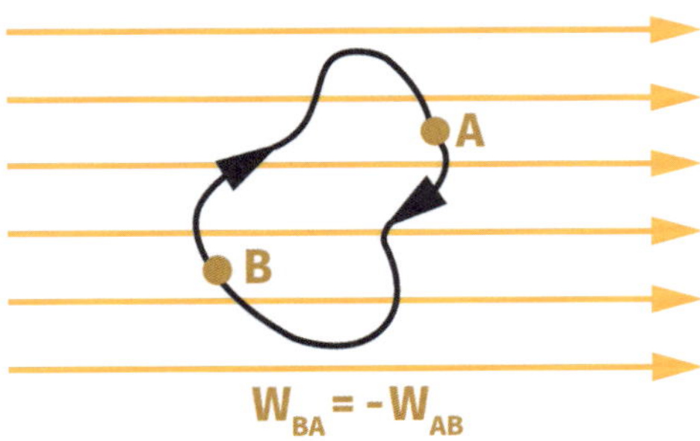

Along a closed curve

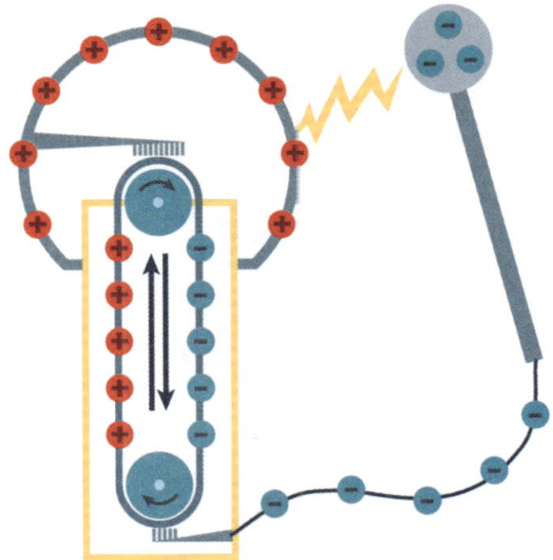

Van de Graaff generator

VISUALISATION

For demonstrating certain electrical phenomena, the Van de Graaff generator can be used, the voltage of which – with respect to the ground (i.e., potential) – can exceed several thousands of volts. However, this does not pose any danger, as only a charge of 10^{-7}-10^{-6} C is stored in it, even if it is well charged.

27

STORAGE FOR THE CHARGES

A device that stores many charges in a small space is the capacitor. When a capacitor is charged, its voltage increases in direct proportion to the amount of charge. The quotient of this amount of charge and the voltage produced is the charge-carrying capacity or capacitance, denoted by C=Q/U; its unit of measurement is the farad (F).

IN THE JAR

The first capacitor was the so-called **Leyden jar**. This is a glass vessel, coated with metal inside and outside, i.e., **two metal bodies separated by insulating material**. Legend has it that a German professor once told his students: "A Leyden jar will knock an ox on the ground, and it strikes a man dead". He then grabbed the jar in an improper way and was knocked to the ground, much to the amusement of the audience.

Leyden jar

ON PLATES

The simplest form of capacitor is the plate capacitor: **two parallel metal plates with the same area**. The capacitance of the capacitor (**C**) depends on the surface area (**A**) of the two parallel conductors, the thickness (**d**) of the insulating material between them, and its permittivity (**ε**).

$$C = \varepsilon \cdot \frac{A}{d}$$

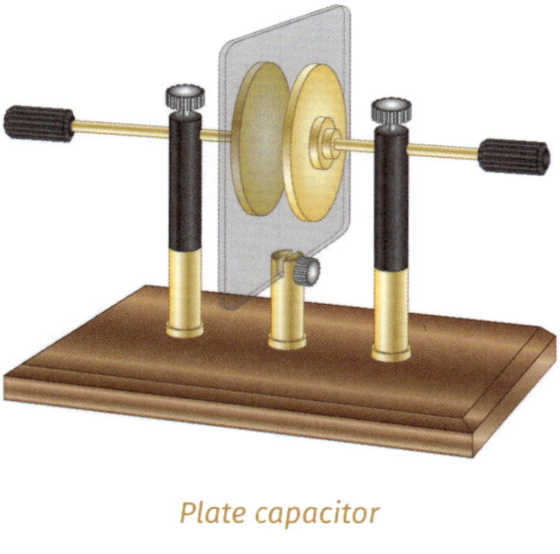

Plate capacitor

IN COMPACT FORM

If 1-2 cm wide and several metres long strips of aluminium foil are insulated from each other with very thin paper and then rolled up, a **paper capacitor** with a relatively large capacitance is obtained that takes up little space. **Electrolytic capacitors** with very large capacitance have a similar structure. Here, one electrode is a liquid (electrolyte), the other is the aluminium foil, and the insulator is the oxide layer formed on the foil surface.

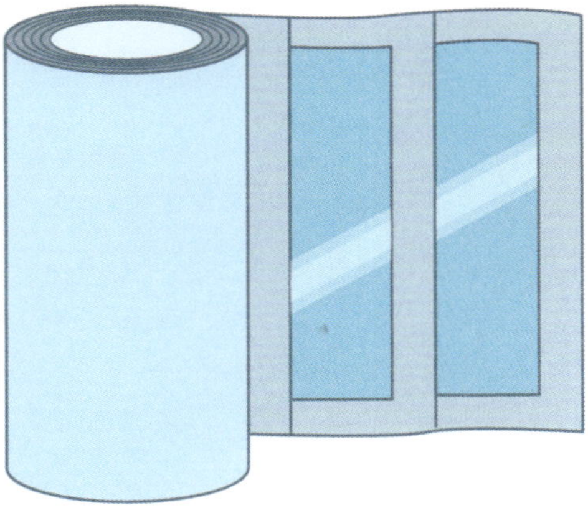

In rolled-up form

LARGE AND SMALL

The value of 1 F is a very high capacity. In practice, only fractions of it are used, namely pico- (10^{-12}) and nano- (10^{-9}), and for electrolytic capacitors micro- (10^{-6}) and millifarad (10^{-3}). The latest carbon-based electrical double-layer capacitors can achieve capacitance up to 5000 F, but since they only have a voltage of about 1 V, further development is required.

Through-hole and surface mounted capacitors

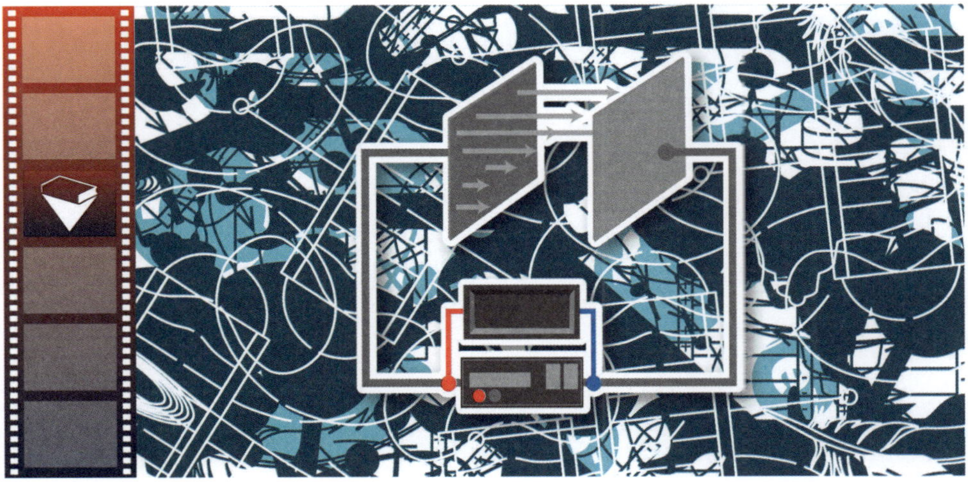

28

CHARGES IN MOTION

Charged bodies in an electric field are subject to forces. This allows them to move, resulting in different conduction phenomena. This can happen in different media, e.g., in metallic conductors, in gases or ionic solutions, or even in air. Positive charges (such as protons) move in the direction of the electric field, while negative charges (such as electrons) move in the opposite direction.

THE ELECTRIC CURRENT

Under the influence of an external field, **charged particles** will move in an ordered way, which is called electric current. Its intensity is indicated by the amount of charge that flows through a certain cross-section within a unit of time.

Symbol: I, magnitude: $I = \frac{\Delta Q}{\Delta t}$

Where **ΔQ** is the amount of charge that flows through the entire cross-section of the conductor in a time **Δt**.

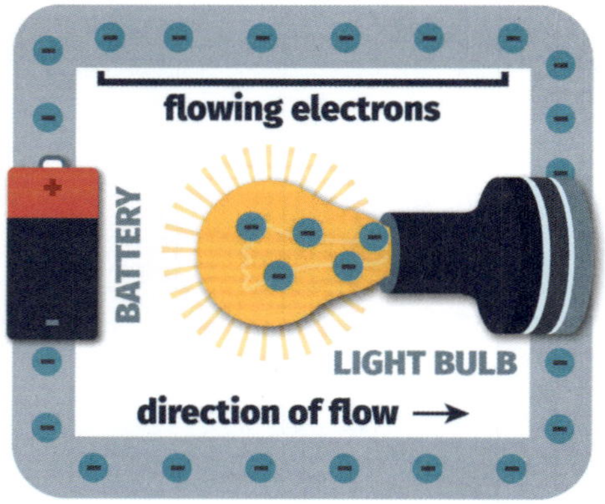

Simple circuit

A CURRENT OF 50 mA CAN BE FATAL

VALUE

The unit of **electric current** is the **ampere**, its symbol is **A**. In case of a current of **1 A**, a charge of **1 C** passes through the cross-section of the conductor in **1 s**. The **direction of the current** was agreed to be the direction of flow of positive charges, i.e., the direction of the field. Only later was it discovered that the charge carriers that can actually move in metals are the negatively charged electrons, the **flow direction** of which is opposite to that previously assumed. In metallic bonds, valence electrons can be set in motion using a small amount of energy.

DIRECTION

Traditionally, the flow of positive charges (more precisely, the opposite direction to the flow of electrons) is still considered the direction of current. However, also an electric field can cause charged ions to move in gases and liquids. The **flow of charge** can be constant and stationary, or variable over time, like in lightning or sparks.

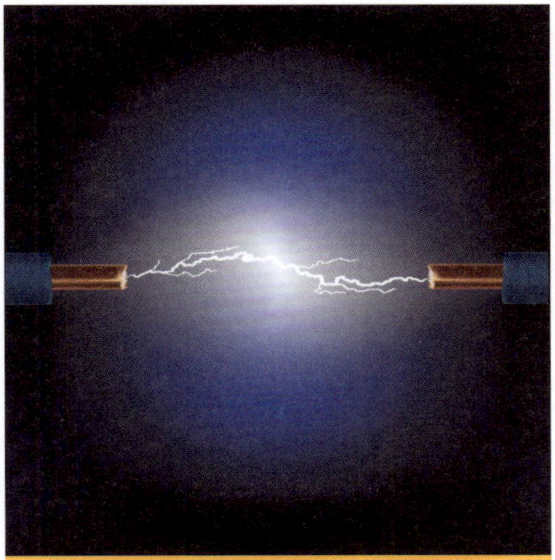

Electrical breakdown

EFFECT

Phenomena produced by electric current can also be observed frequently in our environment. In most cases it is the purpose for which the electricity is actually used, in other cases it is a side effect. Electric current produces heat, creates a magnetic field, causes chemical changes, and can also produce movement or light. But we should always be careful, since electricity flowing through the human body can cause injuries or even death.

Application of generated heat

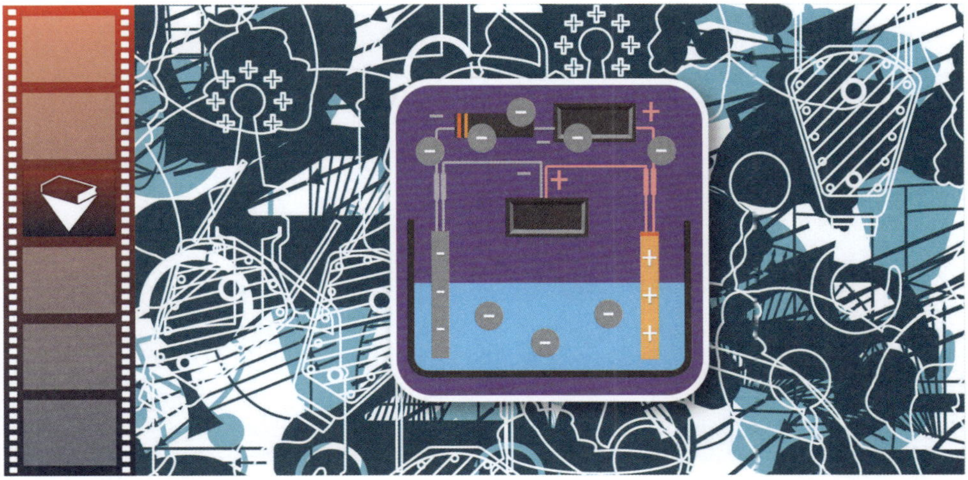

29 ELECTROLYSIS

Solutions or melts of acids, bases, or salts are called electrolytes because due to their free-moving ions they have better electrical conductivity than e.g., distilled water. Electrolysis is an electrochemical process that takes place in an electrolyte under the influence of electric current. An electrolyte can also be easily made at home, by dissolving table salt in water.

DISSOCIATION

Electrolytic dissociation is the process by which table salt (**NaCl**) poured into water breaks down into positive sodium and negative chlorine ions. The current generated in the electrolyte is the result of ion migration: ions of different charges migrate to the electrode with the opposite charge, where they neutralise, and deposit usually as a gas or a solid material.

CHARGE OF AN ION

The charge of an ion is obtained by dividing the amount of charge carried by the circuit by the number of ions extracted. Experience shows that the charge obtained this way is always an integral multiple (**n**) of a given value (the elementary charge, $e = 1.6 \cdot 10^{-19}$ C), where q_{ion} is the charge of an ion, **Q** is the total charge carried by a current **I** in time **t**, and N_{ion} is the number of ions.

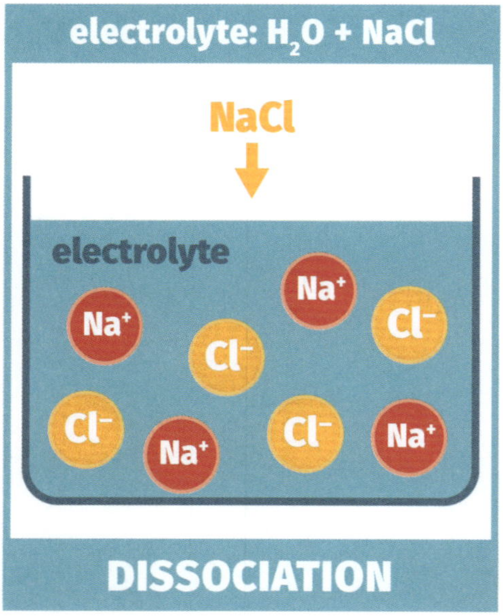

$$q_{ion} = \frac{Q}{N_{ion}} = \frac{I \cdot t}{N_{ion}} = n \cdot 1.6 \cdot 10^{-19}\,C$$

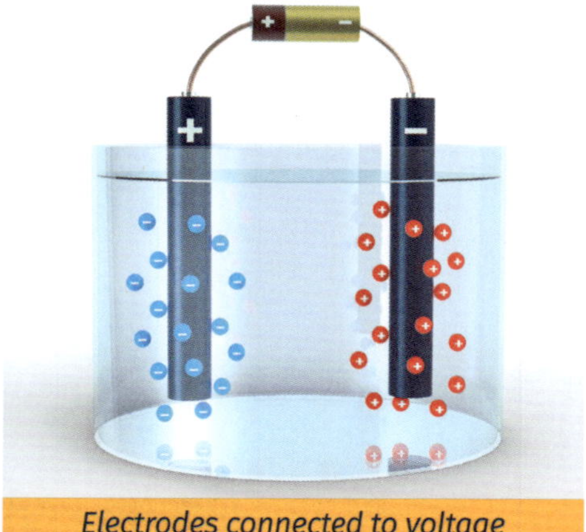

Electrodes connected to voltage

FARADAY'S LAWS OF ELECTROLYSIS

Faraday's first law states the mass of material deposited at the electrodes at current **I** and time **t** is: **$m=k \cdot I \cdot t$**, where **k** is a constant dependent on the material, called the electrochemical equivalent, which represents the mass of material deposited by a unit charge. According to the **second law**, the amount of material **n** deposited is proportional to the amount of charge and inversely proportional to the **chemical valence** of the material (**z**).

$$n=\frac{I \cdot t}{F \cdot z}$$, **where F is the Faraday constant (approx. 96 485 C/mol)**

Thus, to deposit one mole of a substance, a charge of 96 485 C times the chemical valence of the substance is required.

UTILISATION

Electrolysis can be used, for example, for electroplating: a process during which a thin metal coating is produced on the surface of another metal. The purpose may be corrosion protection, increasing wear resistance, conductivity, or solderability, or simply decoration.

Galvanised screws

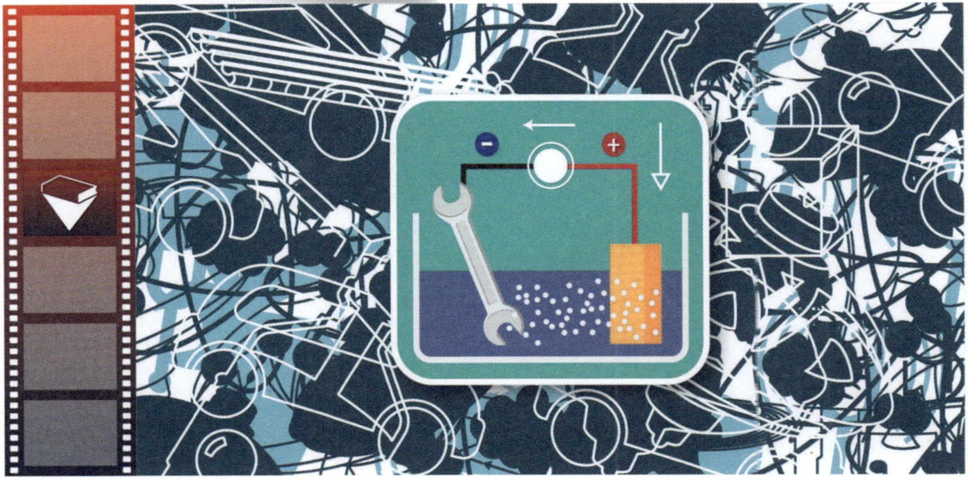

30 CURRENT IN GAS

Being a gaseous substance itself, air is an excellent electrical insulator, like gases in general. The reason for this is that air contains only a few free charge carriers (ions, electrons), which are mainly generated by the ionising effect of solar and cosmic radiation. If there is only a weak electrical effect in the air, the flow of ions is negligible.

IONISATION

A strong electric field accelerates ions to such an extent that when they collide with neutral atoms, they ionise them, creating new free charge carriers. This phenomenon is called collision ionisation and can occur in the form of **spark discharges**, **arc discharges** or **lightning**, depending on the amount of charge.

Arc welding with electric arc

LIGHT

Only if they have sufficient kinetic energy can ions moving in a gas ionise other neutral particles. This can be achieved by increasing either the accelerating electric, or the distance between two collisions so that the ions can accelerate more. The mean **free path** can be increased by reducing the number of particles, i.e., by using a rarefied gas. In gas discharge lamps, for example, a rarefied gas is used that glows when the electrodes connected to the ends of the tube are energised. This phenomenon is called **glow discharge**.

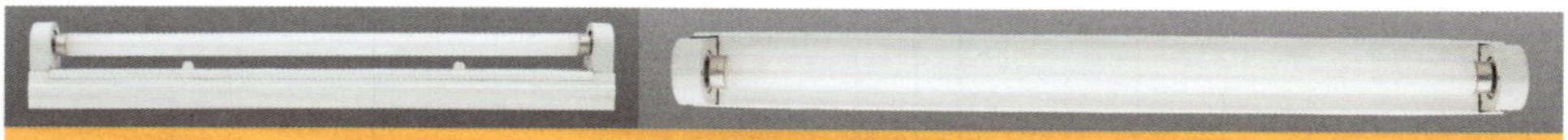

Low-pressure fluorescent tubes

DISCHARGE

Before the **formation of bolts of lightning**, clouds go through a charge separation process: usually the lower part of the cloud becomes negatively charged and the upper part positively charged. When the potential difference between the ground and the lower part of the cloud exceeds a certain limit, the electrons flow towards the surface of the earth in the form of an electrical discharge and the lightning strikes the ground. Usually currents of 10 to 100 thousand amperes are generated, which transfer a charge of 1 to 2 C in a fraction of a second.

IONISATION

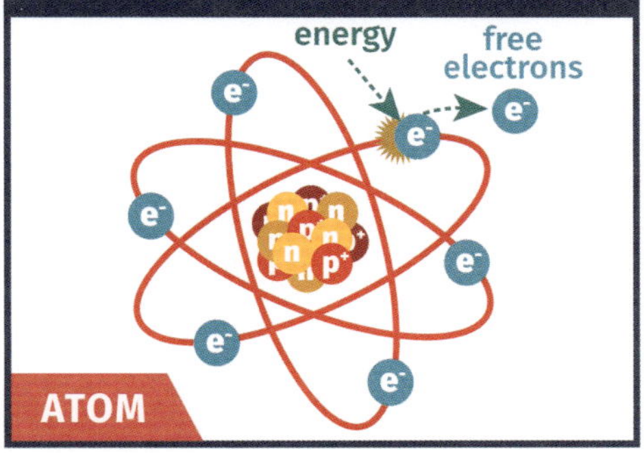

SOUND

Along the route of the lightning, the molecules of the air are ionised, which is accompanied by an intense light effect. Thunder is caused by the expansion of the suddenly heated air, which creates a shock wave with a strong sonic effect. Lightning does not always strike objects on the ground, but often also neighbouring clouds, in which case the lightning is usually horizontal.

CONDUCTION IN GASES IS A CHAIN REACTION

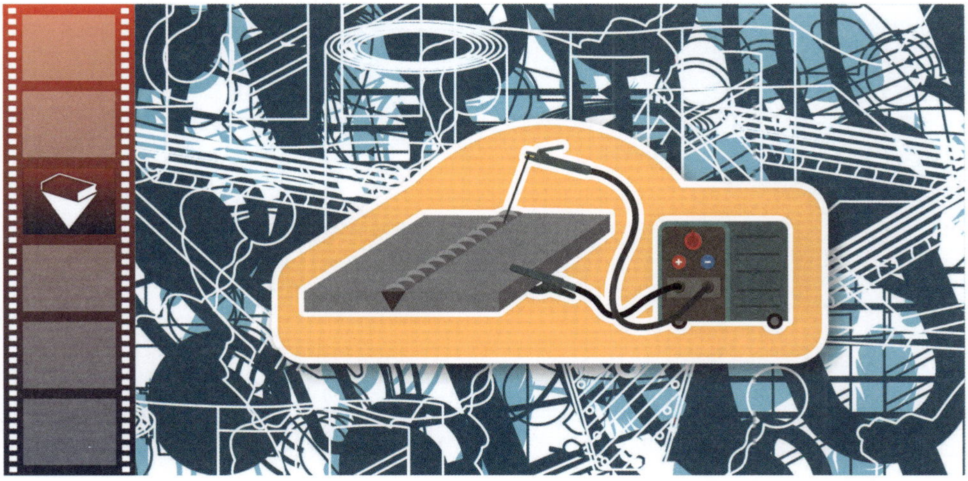

31 CIRCUIT MADE SIMPLE

The electric field exerts a force on a charged body or particle. If a voltage is created between the endpoints of a substance that can conduct electricity, a charge flow, or current, is created in the wire.

THE MAIN PARTS

To maintain the voltage difference needed for the flow of charges, some kind of **power source** is required. In our everyday life, we usually use a mains power source, an accumulator, or a battery for this purpose. An **electrical load** is an appliance or device that we want to operate with the help of electricity. The power source and the load connected by a **wire** form a circuit that can be broken by a specially designed device, the switch.

THE CIRCUIT OF ELECTRICITY

The power source converts various types of energy into electricity and the load converts it back into mechanical, chemical, or thermal energy. The conductor takes care of transporting the electricity. Bear in mind that **grid electricity** is not a direct current but an alternating current, so the direction of the current changes periodically, 50 times per second in our country.

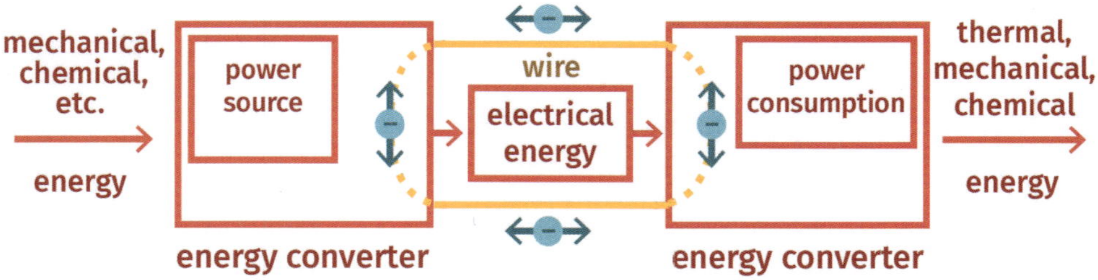

Before and after conversion

MEASUREMENT AT THE ELECTRICAL LOAD

The **voltage meter** or voltmeter measures the voltage between two points in the circuit. Thus, if we want to measure the voltage at the load, the device must be connected in parallel to its two terminals. The **ammeter** is used to measure the current flowing through the load and must therefore be connected in series in the same branch of the circuit.

A multimeter can measure both voltage and current

OHM'S LAW

*The results of voltage and current measurements show a direct proportionality: the constant value **U/I** is independent of the voltage connected to the load or the current flowing through it and is specific to the load. This constant is called electrical resistance; its symbol is **R**. The unit of resistance is the ohm, the symbol of which is: **Ω**. The resistance of an electrical component is **1 Ω** when a current of **1 A** flows through it at a voltage of **1 V**.*

Ohm's-law-triangle

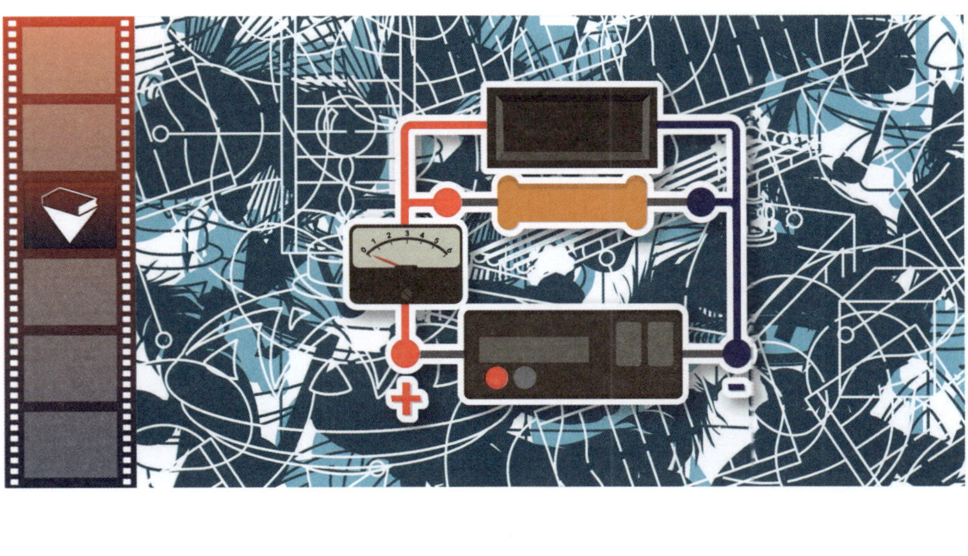

32 OBSTACLE FOR THE CURRENT

Let's measure the resistance of metal wires of different lengths (l), cross-sections (A), and material qualities, i.e., electrical resistivities (ρ (rho)) at a constant temperature. At constant voltage, the current flowing through a conductor (I) is directly proportional to the cross-section of the conductor and inversely proportional to its length.

RESISTANCE

The resistance of a wire is described by the following equation, where **ρ** is a proportionality factor, characteristic of the conductor material:

$$R = \frac{U}{I} = \rho \cdot \frac{l}{A}$$

The **electrical resistivity** gives the resistance of a 1 m long material with a cross-section of 1 m^2. The unit is **Ωm**. The value of the electrical resistivity for conductors is about 10^{-8} - 10^{-4} Ωm, and for insulators 10^{8} - 10^{15} Ωm. The unit used in practice is usually the following:

$$\frac{\Omega \cdot mm^2}{m} = 10^{-6}\,\Omega m$$

Use as a heater coil

$$I \sim \frac{A}{l}$$

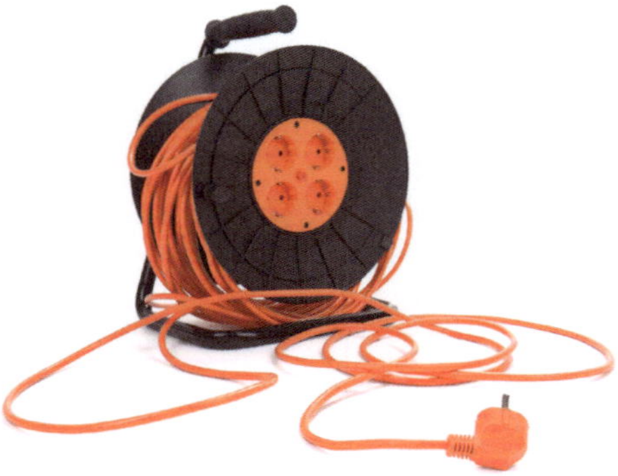

Longer and thus has a higher resistance

HEATING EFFECT

In **metallic conductors**, the so-called conducting electrons move at a uniform average velocity at constant temperature and voltage. However, as the temperature rises, their movement is increasingly impeded by metal ions moving with increased intensity, so the average velocity of the electrons decreases, thereby increasing the resistance of the metal.

DIRECTLY

One of the functions of **multimeters** allows for measuring resistance directly. The basic unit, which is supplied with an auxiliary voltage and can be used to measure current, is connected in series with an appropriately set potentiometer and the unknown resistor. In this case, the scale of the unit can be set according to the value of the resistance. If the **series-connected ohmmeter** is short-circuited, zero will be displayed, and if its terminals are empty, an infinite value will appear.

Analogue multimeter

AT -273 °C

*The average velocity of the electrons involved in conduction can be increased considerably, i.e., the resistance can be decreased, if the thermal movement of the ions in the metal grid is reduced. At temperatures close to **0 K**, the resistance of a pure metallic conductor free of external atoms approaches zero. This phenomenon is called superconductivity.*

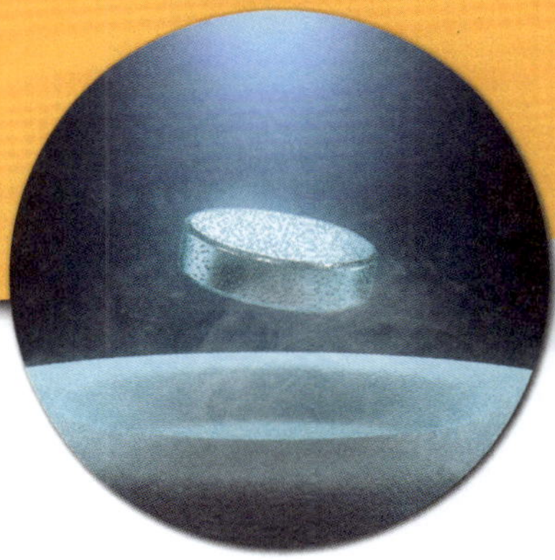

Magnet floats above the superconductor

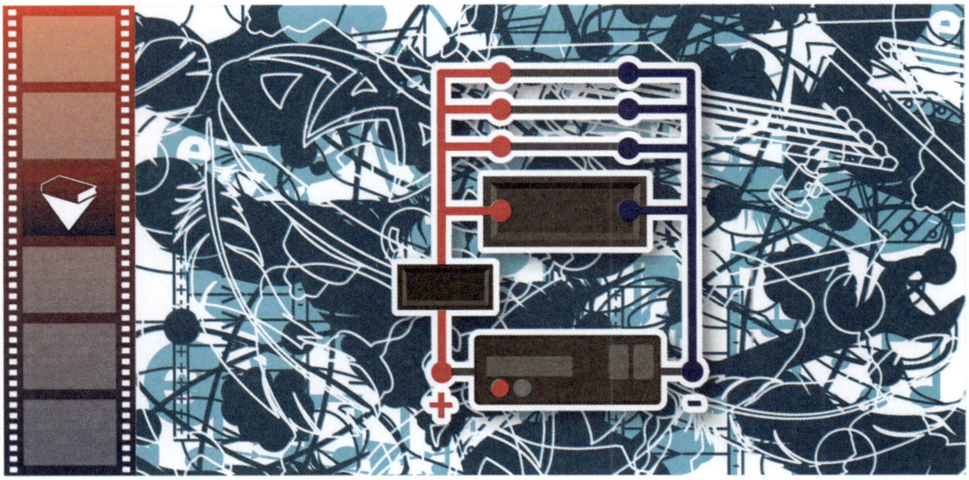

33 WITH SEVERAL LOADS

Several loads can be connected to circuits at a time. There are two ways to do this: in parallel or in series. The result is also different: with series connection the voltage, while in parallel, the current flowing in the circuit is distributed across the resistors.

IN SERIES

In a circuit connected in series, the **loads**, which can generally be characterised as resistors, **are connected without any branching**. No other element is connected to their connection points. An ohmmeter connected in parallel with them when measuring is not considered a load because of its high internal resistance.

Nice and orderly in series

EQUAL CURRENT

Two (or more) resistors connected in series have the same current flowing through them (**$I=I_1=I_2$**). However, the magnitude of the voltage across each resistor depends on the magnitude of their resistance and – in accordance with **Kirchhoff's loop rule** – their sum is equal to the voltage of the battery (**$U_0=U_1+U_2$**). If the voltages are divided by the same current, the resultant is the sum of the individual resistances, i.e., **$R_t=R_1+R_2$** and is thus always greater than the value of each individual resistance.

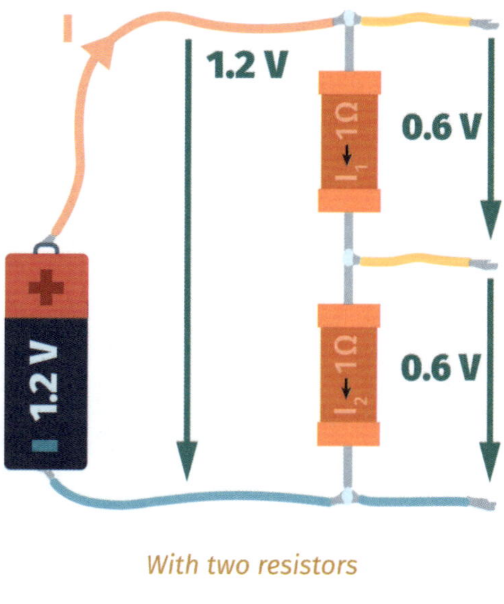

With two resistors

EQUAL VOLTAGE

A circuit connected in parallel can be composed by connecting both terminals of two (or more) components to the two terminals of the battery. In this case, the loads have the same voltage (**$U_0 = U_1 = U_2$**), but their current is inversely proportional to their resistance.

$$I_1 = \frac{U_1}{R_1} \quad \text{and} \quad I_2 = \frac{U_2}{R_2}$$

According to **Kirchhoff's junction rule**, the sum of the currents is equal to the current of the main branch (**$I_t=I_1+I_2$**).

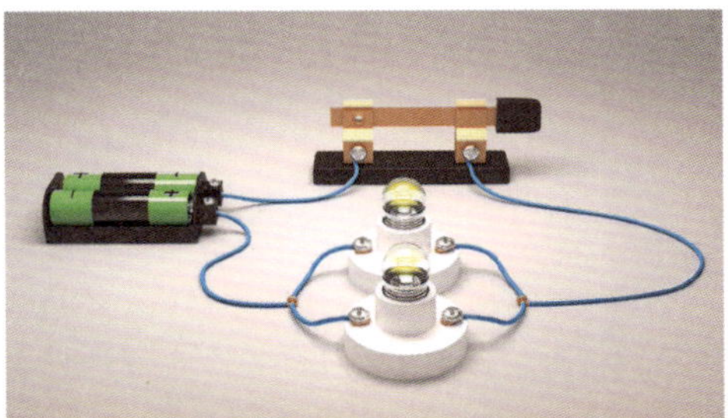

With two common connections

SIMPLIFIED

$$\frac{U_0}{R_t} = \frac{U_1}{R_1} + \frac{U_2}{R_2}$$

*After using the equation **$I_t=I_1+I_2$** and doing simplification, the following relation is obtained for the total resistance:*

$$\frac{1}{R_t} = \frac{1}{R_1} + \frac{1}{R_2}$$

That is, the reciprocal of the total resistance is equal to the sum of the reciprocals of the individual resistances. After a small transformation, the connection can also be expressed this way:

$$R_t = \frac{R_1 \cdot R_2}{R_1 + R_2}$$

*which can be denoted after simplification: **$R_t=R_1 \times R_2$**. The total resistance in a parallel circuit is always smaller than the value of the individual resistances.*

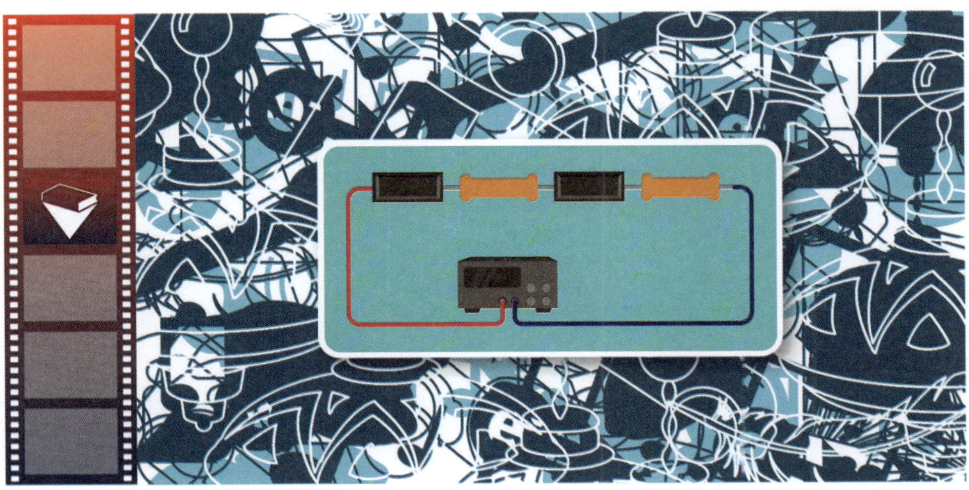

34 SHORT-CIRCUIT VS OPEN-CIRCUIT

The operation of an electrical circuit requires a device that maintains a steady flow of charge from location with the higher potential towards the location with the lower potential. This requires the realisation of an opposite movement of charges within the device. This is called charge separation. The energy required for the separation is provided by the generator (current or voltage source).

OPEN-CIRCUIT

The **open-circuit voltage** or **electromotive force** (**emf**) of a power source is the maximum voltage that can be measured when the power source is unloaded. The symbol of the open-circuit voltage is **ε**, its unit measurement is **volt** (**V**). For an accurate measurement, a voltmeter with the highest possible internal resistance is required.

9 V – without load

THE SHORT CIRCUIT IS DANGEROUS

INTERNAL

The generator also has an internal resistance R_{int}. The external resistance R_{ext} of the operated circuit elements together with the internal resistance determines the current in the circuit. The open-circuit voltage is therefore the sum of the terminal voltage U_{ext} at the external circuit elements and the voltage U_{int} at the internal resistance: $\varepsilon = U_{ext} + U_{int}$.

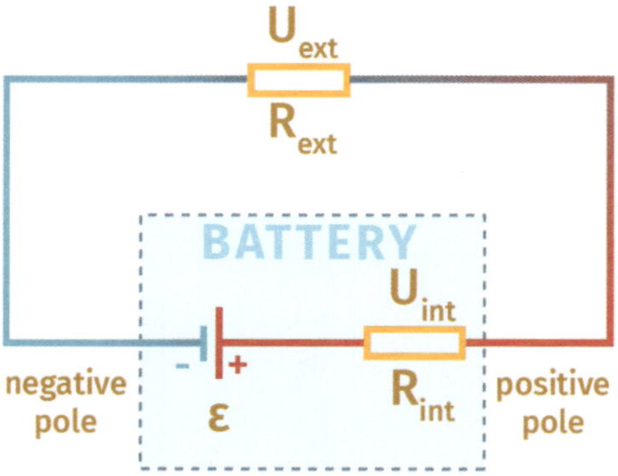

Between the terminals

THE LOSS

If the internal resistance is negligible compared to the total resistance R_{ext} of the components, the open-circuit voltage is equal to the terminal voltage. An open circuit means that the circuit is interrupted. R_{ext} can thus be assumed to be infinitely large, so that the total voltage appears at the terminals. **The internal resistance characterises the loss of the generator in the form of heat.** Therefore, only the terminal voltage appears at the load, which can be much lower than the open-circuit voltage, depending on the load.

Cooling is required

THE FAILURE

The highest current flows if a short-circuit is created ($R_{ext}=0$) the magnitude of which is:

$$I_s = \frac{\varepsilon}{R_{int}}$$

As suddenly a high current flows through the wire, it can overheat, melt, or even cause a fire. In order to protect the components against the short-circuit current, a device must be applied to break the circuit when a large current surge occurs (e.g., fuses, or circuit breakers).

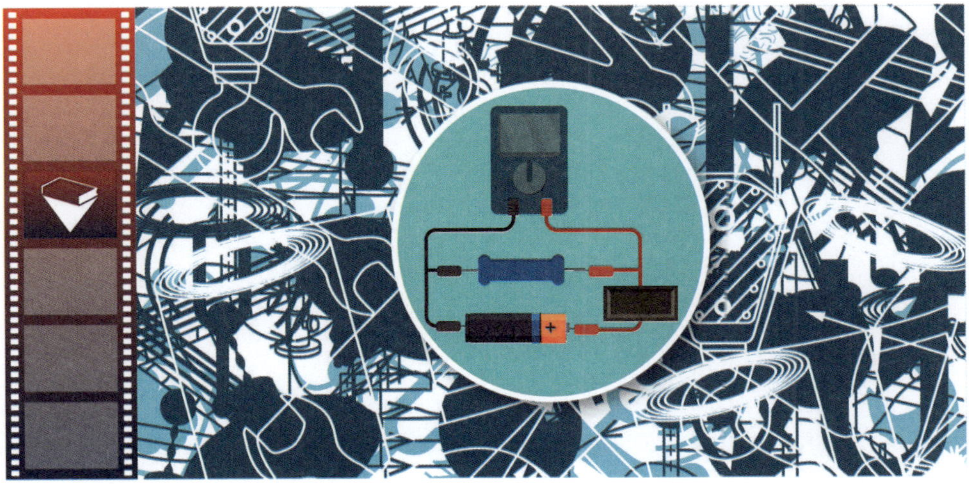

35

THE CONDUCTOR AS A MAGNET

Experiments show that both permanent magnets and current-carrying conductors are surrounded by a magnetic field. This field rotates the compass needle and the current-carrying conductor frame, as well as deflects moving charges.

MAGNETIC FIELD

The magnitude of the magnetic field **B** around a straight conductor depends on the current **I**, the distance **r** from the conductor and the μ_r relative permeability of the material filling the space. In addition, its value is also influenced by the μ_0 constant, called the permeability of vacuum.

$$B = \mu_0 \cdot \mu_r \cdot \frac{I}{2 \cdot r \cdot \pi}, \text{ where } \mu_0 = 4 \cdot \pi \cdot 10^{-7} \frac{Vs}{Am}$$

The magnetic field vector around a straight conductor at a certain point is the tangent of the field line (circle) passing through this point. Its direction can be determined with the right-hand rule: If the thumb points in the direction of the current, the other closed fingers point in the direction of the induction.

IN A STRAIGHT COIL CARRYING A CURRENT, THE MAGNETIC FIELD IS HOMOGENEOUS

WHICH WAY DOES IT MOVE?

When a current-carrying conductor is placed in a magnetic field, it is subject to a force, whose value reaches its maximum when the magnetic field is perpendicular to it. Let's turn our left hand with the palm facing the magnetic field lines so that the four fingers point in the direction of the current. Our thumb then points in the direction of the force acting on the conductor, called the **Lorentz force** (F_{Lor}). From this, we can also deduce the direction of the coil rotation in the magnetometer during the measurement.

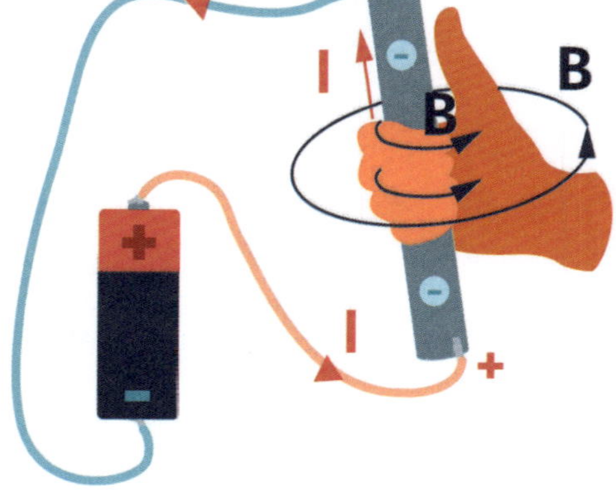

Right-hand rule

EVEN BIGGER

In the case of coils, the magnitude of the magnetic field is **directly proportional** to the current **I** flowing through them and the number of turns **N**, but inversely proportional to the length of the coil **l**. For a coil placed in a vacuum:

$$B = \mu_0 \cdot \frac{I \cdot N}{l}$$

If the inside of the coil is not filled with vacuum but some material, its relative permeability must be taken into account. This shows you how many times the induction of the magnetic field filled with the given material grows relative to the vacuum.

$$B = \mu_0 \cdot \mu_r \cdot \frac{I \cdot N}{l}$$

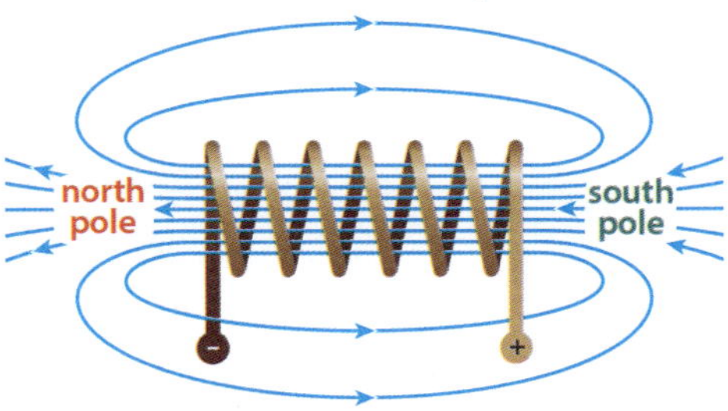

Magnetic field of a current-carrying coil

WITH IRON CORE

*Materials with high relative permeability are called **ferromagnets**. Iron, for example, has a relative permeability of about 2000, so the magnetic field of a coil with an iron core is 2000 times higher that without an iron core. A coil with a soft iron core is an electromagnet, which has the advantage over a permanent magnet with its magnetic effect that can be switched off by disconnecting it from the current.*

Lifting with an electromagnet

36 BETWEEN THE ENDS

Let's move a metal rod of length l with a velocity v in a magnetic field B in a way that l, B, and v are perpendicular to each other pairwise. The Lorentz force (F_{Lor}) acts on the free charges inside the metal rod in the direction of the rod. This sets the electrons in motion so that one end of the rod becomes negatively charged because of the excess of electrons, and the other end becomes positively charged because of the shortage of electrons.

THE FIELD

The attractive electrostatic force (**F_{el}**) exerted on the charges by the resulting electric field **E** is opposite to the Lorentz force. Charge separation lasts only until these two forces cancel each other out: **$F_{Lor}=F_{el}=Q\cdot v\cdot B=Q\cdot E$**, from which **$v\cdot B=E$**. This means that a homogeneous electric field is induced in the rod, which depends on the magnetic field and the speed of movement.

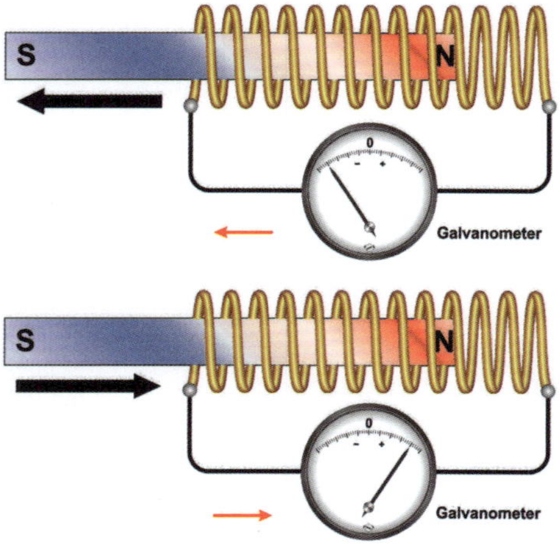

The magnet moves in the coil

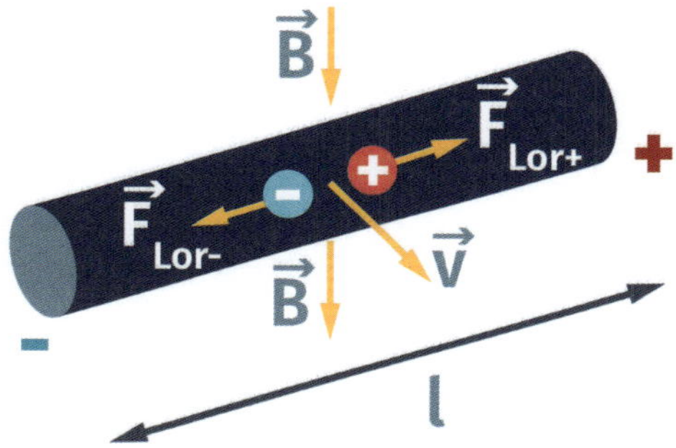

The conductor moves in the magnetic field

INDUCTION THROUGH MOTION

The **voltage between the ends of the rod** when **v** and **B** are perpendicular to each other is **$U=E\cdot l=v\cdot B\cdot l$**. If **v** and **B** are not perpendicular but form an angle **α**, only the component of the velocity perpendicular to **B** is to be considered, i.e., **$U=v\cdot B\cdot l\cdot \sin\alpha$**. The movement of a single conductor produces only a small voltage, but when a coil with several turns moves in a perpendicular magnetic field, the induced voltage is multiplied by the number of turns. Voltage is not only induced when the coil moves, but also when the magnetic field changes.

LAW

The direction of the induced current due to the induced voltage in a conductor moving in the magnetic field is such that its effect opposes the movement. This is **Lenz's law**. This rule, discovered by the Estonian-born German physicist Emil Lenz (1804-1865), is essentially an expression of the general empirical law of conservation of energy.

Heinrich Friedrich Emil Lenz

APPLICATION

Coils can be used to generate magnetic fields and also voltages. For example, the rotating coil of a generator produces a variable magnetic field, while induced voltage is developed between the terminals of its stationary coil.

Generator

37 STANDING STILL

When the conductor and the magnetic field move relative to each other, this causes a charge movement and induces voltage in the conductor. This is called motional electromotive force (emf). The phenomenon of transformer emf occurs when the conductor itself is at rest, but the magnetic field around it changes over time.

CHANGE

When the magnetic field (**B**) in a coil connected to a circuit is changed, **the change in magnetic flux** (**Φ=B·A,** where **A** is the cross-section) **in the coil induces a voltage in the coil**. The change in magnetic flux in the coil (**ΔΦ**) – and thus the voltage measured at the coil terminals – can also be brought about by placing a second coil near the first one on a common axis and changing the current in the second coil.

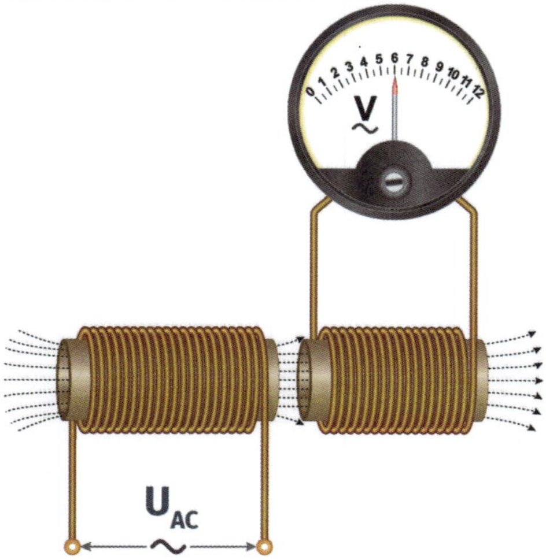

The invisible connection between two coils

WITH ANOTHER COIL

In accordance with Lenz's law, the direction of the induced current is always such that its magnetic field opposes the current-generating flux change. According to **Faraday's law**, the induced voltage is proportional to the change in flux, whereby for a number of turns of **N**, the voltage is induced **N** times.

$$U_i = -N \cdot \frac{\Delta\Phi}{\Delta t}$$

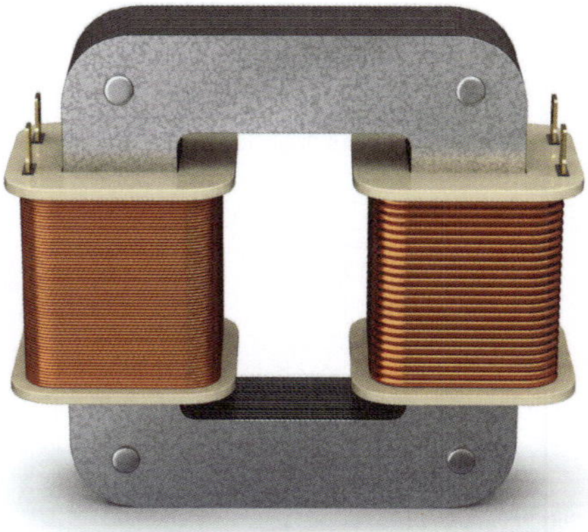

Transformer

SELF-INDUCTANCE

When the current **I** flowing in a coil is changed – e.g., by switching the connected power source on or off – the magnetic field inside the coil changes, which produces an induced voltage in the coil itself due to the transformer emf. This is called **self induction**. According to Lenz's law, the induced voltage inhibits the change, either by delaying the current when it is switched on or by maintaining it for a certain time when it is switched off, where **L** is the inductance of the coil.

$$U_i = -L \cdot \frac{\Delta I}{\Delta t}$$

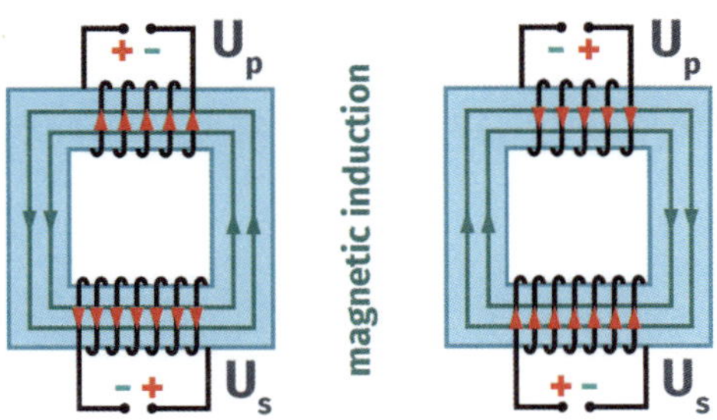

Working principle of a transformer

CANCELLED OUT

If a coil is made so that half the turns are wound in one direction and the other in the opposite direction, the same induction is developed, but with different directionality. The two therefore cancel each other out and no magnetic effect occurs in the vicinity of the coils. The bifilar winding is therefore not used to make inductive coils, but induction-free resistors.

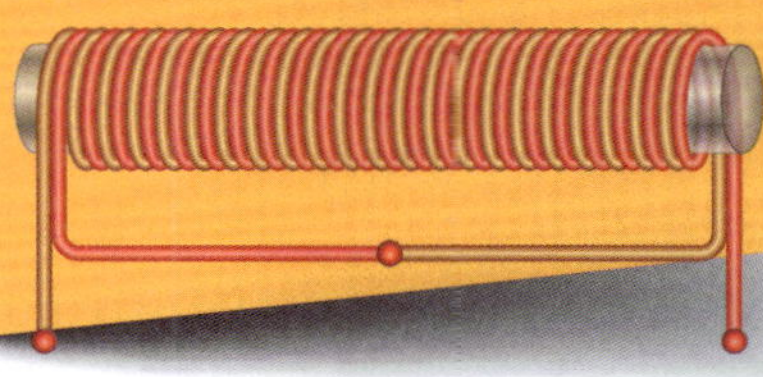

THE MAGNETISM OF THE COIL HAS A FEEDBACK EFFECT ON ITSELF

38 CURRENT BACK AND FORTH

When the current flow of charge carriers in a conductor varies over time, it is called a variable current. A common case of this is alternating current (AC), where both the direction and the strength of the current change periodically. Based on the variation of the instantaneous values of the current over time, a distinction is made between currents with sinusoidal, rectangular, trapezoidal, and triangular characteristics.

APPLICATION

Alternating current is also used in households. In the British power grid, the **frequency of the alternating current is 50 Hz** and varies according to a sine function. This means that the current changes its direction 100 times per second according to the sinusoidal feature. To generate an alternating current, an alternating voltage is required.

From the electrical grid

PRODUCTION

Alternating current can be generated in the following way with the help of motional emf. Let us place a conducting frame in a homogeneous magnetic field in an arrangement where it can be rotated about an axis perpendicular to the field lines. Let us connect a centre-zero voltmeter to its two terminals and rotate the frame with a constant angular velocity **ω**. It can be seen that the pointer of the voltmeter is periodically deflected first in one direction and then in the opposite one.

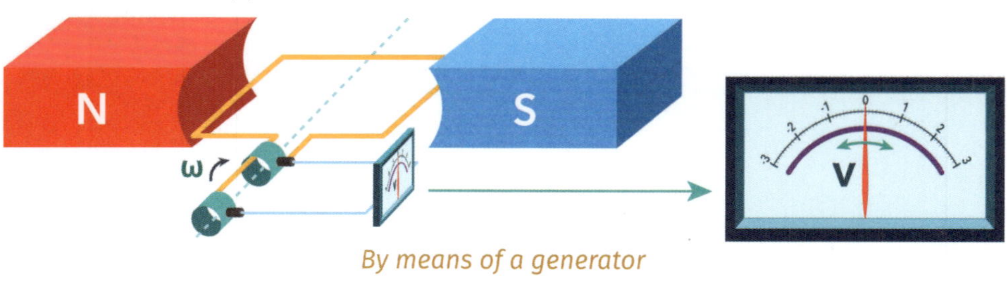

By means of a generator

ROOT MEAN SQUARE VALUE (RMS)

As the instantaneous values of the alternating voltage vary constantly, the term of effective voltage is worth introducing according to the following definition: The RMS value of the alternating voltage is equal to the value of a direct voltage performing the same work at the same resistance in the same time interval. The RMS value of the sinusoidal AC voltage is as follows:

$$V_{RMS} = \frac{V_{peak}}{\sqrt{2}}$$

TEMPORAL PROGRESSION

The edges of length l of the frame move in the magnetic field with a circumferential velocity $v = \omega \cdot r$. Voltage is only induced when the instantaneous velocity has a component perpendicular to the field lines. Thus, when calculating the amount of voltage induced, the velocity only of this component needs to be taken into account: $V_i = B \cdot l \cdot v_\perp = B \cdot l \cdot v \cdot \sin\alpha$. The induced voltage therefore varies sinusoidally. The maximum value is $V_{peak} = B \cdot l \cdot v$. which can be measured in two points in time during one period, with a different sign.

$$\alpha = \frac{\pi}{2} \text{ and } \alpha = \frac{3\pi}{2}$$

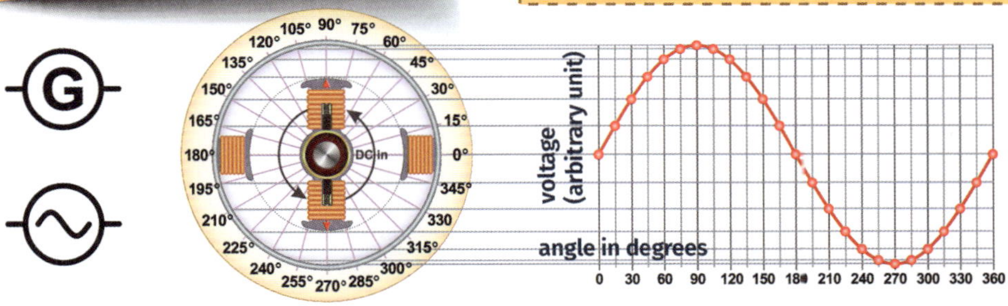

From the circular motion

39

THREE IN SERIES

Let's connect a resistor, a coil, and a capacitor in series. Let's apply an AC voltage to this series RLC circuit, and measure the voltage of the individual elements of the circuit. We can see that the sum of the RMS voltages measured on the individual elements is greater than the RMS value of the voltage connected to the circuit.

THE RESISTOR

The explanation for this **apparent contradiction** is that the phase relation of the voltages at the individual components cannot be derived from the RMS voltages, but this must also be taken into account when applying the loop rule. The resistor is an exception, here the voltage is in phase with the current.

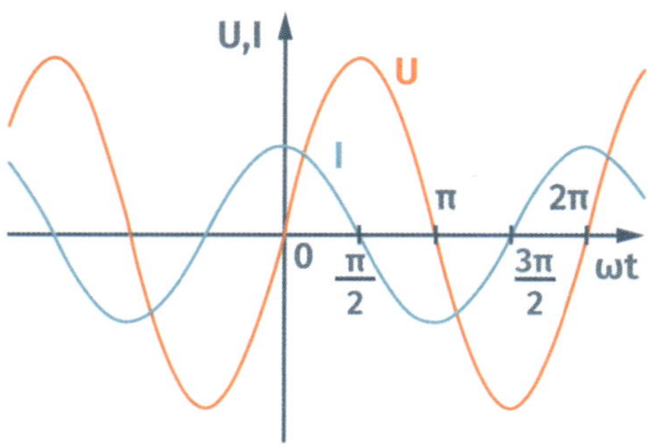

The current leads the way

$$R = \frac{U_R}{I}$$

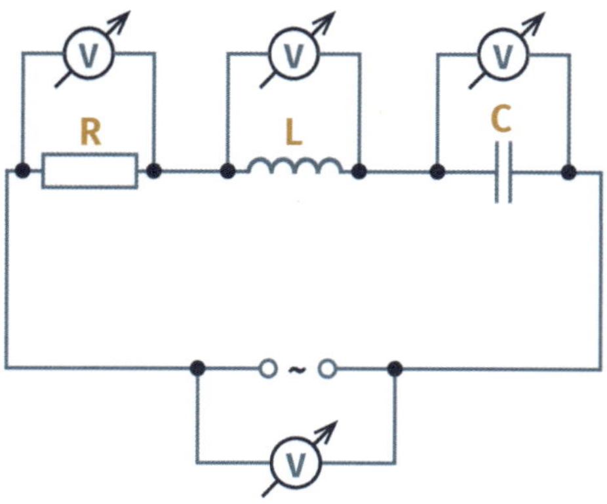

Series RLC circuit

THE CAPACITOR

If an alternating voltage is applied to a capacitor, and the current and voltage in the circuit is plotted as the function of time, it can be seen that the fully charged capacitor delivers the maximum current at the moment when the voltage changes direction. This means that the current does not alternate in phase with the voltage but leads it by 90° ($\pi/2$). **The AC resistance of the capacitor is called the capacitive reactance** and is denoted by X_C.

$$X_C = \frac{U_C}{I}$$ **its unit of measurement: Ω**

THE COIL

When an AC voltage is applied to a coil, the **AC current generates a magnetic field (through induction) in the coil**, which generates an electric field. According to Lenz's law, the electric field opposes the effect that creates it, i.e., it slows down the current, which is thus delayed by 90° compared to the voltage. The AC resistance of the coil is called inductive reactance. Here also applies:

$$X_L = \frac{U_L}{I}$$ **its unit of measurement: Ω**

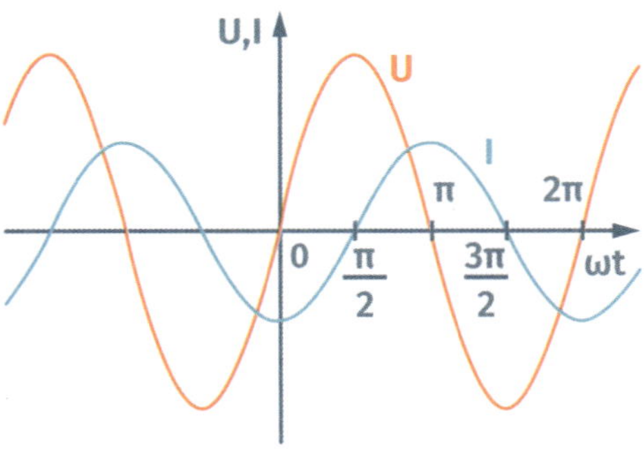

The current is delayed

TOGETHER

*According to the vector representation based on the phase differences and the Pythagorean theorem, $U^2=U_R^2+(U_L-U_C)^2$. Since the current is the same in all components, the current-limiting effect is the impedance (**Z**).*

$$Z=\frac{U}{I}=\sqrt{R^2+(X_L-X_C)^2}$$

The frequency at which the impedance of the circuit is the lowest ($Z_{min}=R$), is called the resonant frequency. Its value is determined by using Thomson's formula:

$$f_0=\frac{1}{2\cdot\pi\cdot\sqrt{L\cdot C}}$$

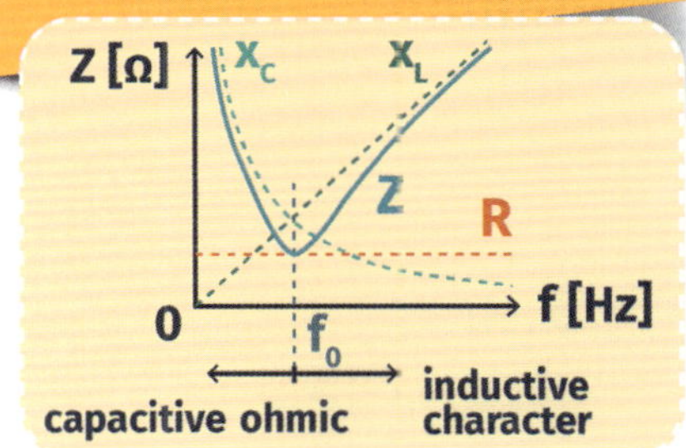

Impedance as a function of frequency

40

PASS ON THE ENERGY

Let's check what happens when a charged capacitor is discharged via a coil. Let's connect an ammeter with a central pointer in the circuit and observe the movement of the pointer. The discharging process is very interesting because the pointer of the meter is periodically deflected first in one direction and then in the opposite.

DISCHARGE

When the circuit is closed, the voltage of the charged capacitor creates a current flow, and this reduces the voltage of the capacitor. The current is also reduced, but this causes a change in the magnetic field of the coil. According to Lenz's law, the changing magnetic field in turn induces a **voltage** in the coil, which **counteracts the decrease in the current**.

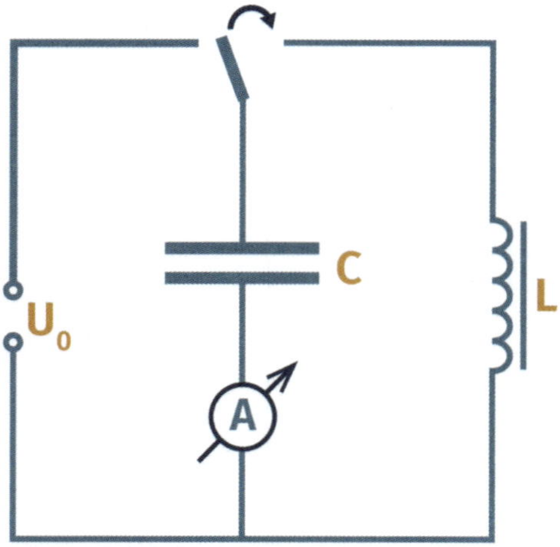

In parallel

THE VIBRATION STARTS

The voltage induced continues to **maintain the original direction of the current**, so that the capacitor is charged again, but now with **reversed polarity**. The process that starts again in the opposite direction is called **electromagnetic oscillation**, and this arrangement is called a **parallel resonance circuit**. If the circuit experiences no external constraints, the resulting vibration is called free electromagnetic oscillation, and the frequency of this oscillation is called eigenfrequency. The amplitude of the vibration will decrease with time due to the losses that occur.

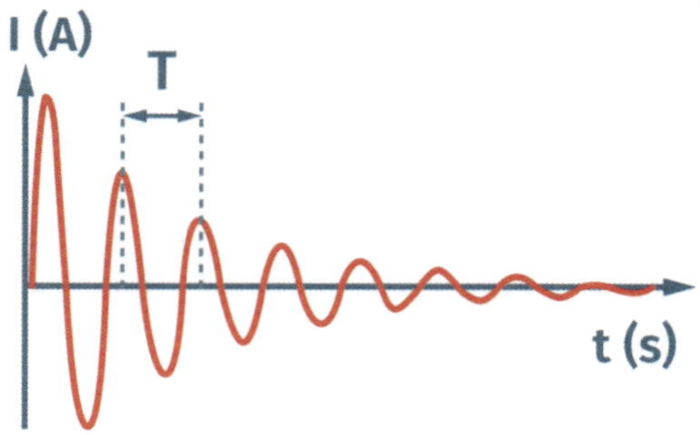

Damped

THE CHARACTERISTIC FREQUENCY

The eigenfrequency of the **LC** resonance circuit with an ideal coil and an ideal capacitor can be easily determined. The voltage at the capacitor is always equal to the voltage at the coil: $U_C = U_L$. If both sides of the equation are divided by the current, the equation for the capacitive and inductive resistance $X_C = X_L$ is obtained.

$$2\pi \cdot f \cdot L = \frac{1}{2\pi \cdot f \cdot C}$$

The natural frequency results from this according to Thomson's formula.

$$f_0 = \frac{1}{2\pi \cdot \sqrt{L \cdot C}}$$

A crystal can also be used instead of a coil

WAVES

In the resonance circuit, the energy from the original electromagnetic field of the capacitor is completely converted into the energy from the magnetic field of the coil and then back again. This parallel circuit is most often found in tuned amplifiers. When the frequency of the incoming signal is equal to the resonant frequency of the resonance circuit, the impedance and therefore the gain of the amplifier is at its maximum.

For tuning

TABLE OF CONTENTS

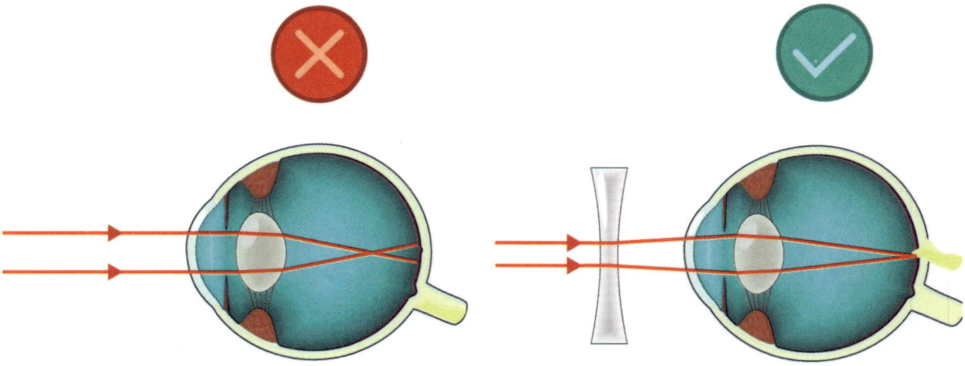